GETTING A CHURCH STARTED
IN THE FACE OF INSURMOUNTABLE ODDS
WITH LIMITED RESOURCES
IN UNLIKELY CIRCUMSTANCES .

GETTING A CHURCH STARTED

IN THE FACE OF INSURMOUNTABLE ODDS

WITH LIMITED RESOURCES

IN UNLIKELY CIRCUMSTANCES

How to establish a church based on a study of 10 new small prospering congregations.

by

by Elmer L. Towns

impact
books

Library of Congress Catalog Card Number: 74-28990
ISBN 0-914850-23-7

CONTENTS

INTRODUCTION 7

THE INCOMPARABLE CHURCH-PLANTER 10

A CHURCH BUILT IN A WAREHOUSE 14

A CHURCH BUILT WITH DIGNITY 27

BEGINNING A CHURCH IN HIS HOME TOWN 37

A GREAT FIRST ANNIVERSARY 48

A CHURCH IN THE LENGTH AND SHADOW OF ITS LEADER 56

THE VALLEY'S MOST EXCITING CHURCH 70

"I WAS NEVER AFRAID OF FAILURE" 81

THE USE OF MONEY IN STARTING A CHURCH 92

A "SWEET, SWEET SPIRIT" COMES OUT OF
 A CHURCH SPLIT 106

THE FASTEST GROWING CHURCH IN RICHMOND 118

GETTING OFF ON THE RIGHT FOOT 128

CHOOSING A LOCATION 137

QUESTIONS ABOUT CHURCH PLANTING 146

CAN A CHURCH START FROM A SPLIT? 162

THE ROLE OF A PIONEER-PASTOR 170

INTRODUCTION

TEN WAYS TO START A CHURCH

Some have asked why such a long title to a book. As I recently scanned titles in a bookstore, I noticed that many titles of Christian books were merely a takeoff on successful secular titles. Also, many other titles were "cute," designed only to catch the eye, but they didn't tell the buyer what was in the book. I wanted a title that would capsulize the thesis of the book because I believe people will read this book for its content when they know its thesis.

Starting a church is exciting, but never an easy task. The miracle of birth is just as evident in church-planting as when a child is born. The world is not hospitable to soul-winning, hence I used the phrase *insurmountable odds*. Most new churches begin with inadequate facilities and limited resources. It almost seems that if they are too financially prosperous, their vitality is not. Like pioneering families, the greatest victories are won only against the most threatening foes. The phrase *unlikely circumstances* was used because there is no ideal place to start a church. The Bible Belt is not ideal because people are gospel-hardened and areas are over-churched. The Catholic neighborhood has a built-in religion barrier; and cold northern cities reject soul-winning churches, calling them religious fanatics. The ten churches in this book were conceived in the heart of their founder and born in adversity. They challenge us to "think the impossible" and "expect the victorious." God still uses those who will passively yield to his plan and tenaciously agonize in work.

Starting new churches is the genius of Christianity. As the population explodes and another community comes into existence, new churches are needed. As old churches lose their fervency and

7

slip into liberalism, new churches are needed to take their place.

Wendell Belew of the Southern Baptist Home Mission Board currently plans 500 new churches in America every year. Someone asks, "What method do you plan to use to plant 500 new churches a year?" He replies, "For 500 churches, we need 500 methods."

There is much truth in Belew's admonition; every community has different needs and every group of people reflects a different composite personality. Each pastor must minister according to his spiritual gifts, hence there is a different application of Biblical principles in every new church.

These churches were chosen because they represented ten geographical sections of America. Also, they were successful in rural, small towns, city and metropolitan areas. These ten men used ten different formulas in building a church. Yet, many of their patterns are similar because there are certain timeless principles that transcend space and culture. These grow out of the nature of the church and the principles used to found churches in the New Testament.

Some of these churches have grown faster than others. None of these churches is perfect—like young children they are growing through the pains of childhood. But even in youth, there is something compelling about a child. Each church, as reflected in each of its pastor-founders, has different strengths, hence each is a different example to guide those building a church.

I don't consider myself an authority on establishing new churches. I have interviewed ten men and have written their stories. They are the authorities; I am simply the channel through which the story is written. My interest in church-founding came after realizing that four of the churches in the book *The Ten Largest Sunday Schools* were begun by the present pastor. Also, I wrote a series on great soul-winning churches in *The Sword of the Lord*. A great number of these also were started by the present pastor. Part of three of these stories (Chapters Seven, Nine, Ten) appeared in *The Sword*, but additional material has been added for this book. The idea for this book came in the spring, 1973, when as Academic Dean of Lynchburg Baptist College, I arranged for a chapel series on "How To Start A Church," and invited eight pastors to share with the student body the lessons they learned. (Four of these chapters were summarized in those chapels.)

When I was a student at Columbia Bible College, South Carolina, I re-organized and pastored the Westminster Presbyterian Church, Savannah, Georgia, (1951-53)—a church building with property but the congregation had gone out of existence. While at Dallas Theological Seminary, I organized and pastored Faith Bible Church (1956-58). It had previously been a Sunday School mission.

Some will not be able to follow the principles of this book and start a successful church because of differing concepts about the church. The end product always determines the process. The end product in this book is a soul-winning, Bible-teaching church that stands for purity, obedience to the Great Commission, and separation from apostasy. Therefore, if this is not the type of church you want to build, all of these principles will not apply to your situation. But, in fact, not all of these principles will apply in any situation. They must be read in light of Scripture, applied in relationship to the community, and integrated by the man of God.

The church is close to the heart of God (Eph. 5:25) and those who start a church have a special place in God's affection. When preaching on the doctrine of the church, I often ask for charter members of that congregation to raise their hands. These, I note, have a special place in God's love for the sacrifice, vision, and labor that brought a church into existence. "One of the greatest privileges in life is to help bring a candlestick (Rev. 2:1,5) into existence, to be there when Christ comes to dwell in a group of people."

Appreciation is offered to the men of these churches who have shared their accomplishments and visions with me. They have read the manuscript to determine its accuracy and given their approval. May God use this manuscript to the extent he has used these churches. And as there is an embryonic world-wide influence in each new convert and new church, may God use this manuscript according to its potential.

ELMER TOWNS
Savannah, Georgia

Spring 1974

CHAPTER ONE

THE INCOMPARABLE CHURCH-PLANTER

God Allows Men to Begin His Church

The man who desires to build a church is usually motivated by the "impossible dream" and he must accomplish the "unperformable task." A church is never a human invention nor is it every man's accomplishment. An *ecclesia* is a people "called out" from sin, beckoned to gather themselves in God's assembly. They are "called out" from normal pursuits to carry out God's commission. The church is established by God, is empowered by God and, ultimately, God is its objective. Those who would start a true church must be motivated by God who is its founder.

The world does not love a church. The system of life is motivated by selfish gains and selfish pleasures. Men obey their natures or mimic the times. Behind the veneer of American life is a system that hates the intrusion of God into its existence. American business is dominated by both moral and immoral men; neither type is usually motivated by the love of Christ. Even though America may have a superior life-style, it still is opposed to the dictates of Christ. A New Testament church convicts the surrounding community by its purity and humility. The world still hates Christian influence. It will not embrace a new church nor will a community naturally support a beginning church. God must perform a miracle each time a new church comes into existence.

Into this improbable situation steps a man. As once "There was a man sent from God whose name was John," (John 1:6), just

11

so God always has a man who will step into the gap (Ezek. 22:30) and respond, "Here am I, send me" (Isa. 6:8).

When the human race was threatened by sexual abuses, God worked through his man—Noah. When the nations were given over to idolatry, God had his man—Abraham. When the world faced seven hard years of famine, God had his man—Joseph. When the people of God were groaning under an oppressive slavery in Egypt, God had his man—Moses. God's man always attempts the unattainable, whether his name is Samuel, David, Nehemiah or Paul.

God still uses a man. One of the greatest tasks a man can do today is start a church. A man begins by obeying God's call. Next he faces his "unattainable task" and in the power of Christ accomplishes a victory a mere individual could never win. He influences his neighborhood, yet must do so in the spirit of humility. He does not desire self-popularization. It is God he magnifies. But when he has successfully accomplished his goal of starting a church, he is both well known and influential. Yet notoriety must never go to his head; to remain influential he must remain humble.

A church is always built by a man, but is never built on a man. Churches started by committees never seem to prosper. God's grace and power must be poured into a man—God's servant. Remember, "A great church is always caused, it never just happens." God always has his servant who sacrifices, prays and works.

James Mastin who drove into Milwaukee with all his furniture loaded on a U-Haul truck appeared about as formidable as David standing before Goliath with five stones. But the thesis of this book is that God still uses the unaided man with limited resources against insurmountable obstacles in unlikely circumstances. Mastin knew no one in the city, had little finances and faced deep religious conviction. Yet, God used James Mastin to build a great church.

Although God does not use a modern Gideon to slay an army of Midianites with 300 faithful soldiers, he still uses the same principle. Jim Singleton went to Tempe, Arizona; Danny Smith to Richmond, Virginia; and the other men of this book have accomplished unthinkable feats. God still uses the unaided man as he used Moses against Egypt, Samson against the Philistines and Joseph to feed a famine-infested world.

None of the church-planters in this book are characterized by great education. They are God's servants and he has given them the wisdom of Proverbs. All of them labor in the spirit of I Corinthians 1:26, 27, "How that not many wise men after the flesh, not many mighty. not many noble are called: But God has chosen the foolish things of the world to confound the wise; and God hath chosen the weak things of the world to confound the things which are mighty." God uses average men to reveal his power.

This volume believes in the vast potential of God's people. When a man is faithful in a small sphere of service, God promotes him to a higher realm of usefulness. In the parable of talents, when the man with five talents was faithful, the Lord gave him five additional talents. Some of the pastors in this book were green and unsure of themselves. I enjoyed watching Carl Godwin grow as he was put under pressure. Each week he is becoming a better preacher. As each man was faithful, God first increased his ability; secondly, God increased the size of his church.

Following the example of these pastors have come their laymen, growing in ability by faithful service. When Jim Histand at Fairfax Baptist Temple had reached 100 through his bus ministry, it was a result of God's increasing his ability and rewarding his faithfulness. His pastor inspired him to accomplishment greater than he ever thought possible.

One of the yet-to-be-revealed influences of these churches is the hundreds of boys who weekly watch their pastor take on unbeatable foes and beat them. Perhaps there are a number of boys in these churches who will be called into service (Timothy) and build greater churches in the future. Just as James Mastin was influenced by Verle Ackerman and the great First Baptist Church of West Hollywood, Florida, there may be a small boy in Milwaukee who will one day build a church greater than either of these.

Dr. G.B. Vick, Pastor of Temple Baptist Church, Detroit, has said, "Great men build great churches while average men serve average churches." If a young man wants to start a church that will be influential, he must study great men. A pastor becomes like the minister he patterns himself after. Some mission churches fail or stagnate because their leaders lack well-balanced spiritual leadership. Simply, the church fails because the leader has not learned the basic steps of Christianity.

To build a great church, a man must have developed a stern hard-headed tenacity. "I'll never give up," Rudy Holland affirmed, banging his fist into the palm of his hand. But the church planter must also nurture the devotional meekness of Puritans. He must have physical endurance to visit sixty hours a week and emotional endurance not to crack when his young converts deny the faith. The pastor-leader must have a reverent sense of spiritual things, yet the cold calculating eye of a businessman. He must be quick to acquire knowledge in a thousand areas where he is ignorant, yet must lead authoritatively for no one else in his congregation knows how to build a church. The pastor-founder must speak persuasively in public and listen sympathetically in private counsel. The man who would establish a church must be an extraordinarily equipped man of deep commitment, iron will, wide scholarship and unblemished experience. If he doesn't have it all when he begins, he must gain it soon and in the acquiring process, he will build a church. If he doesn't personally grow in ratio commensurate to his vision, he will never establish and build the great influential church of his dreams.

As Daniel stood before the lions . . .

As David slew his ten thousands . . .

As Elijah stood alone on Mount Carmel . . .

Today, a young man goes forth to establish a church . . .

CHAPTER TWO

A CHURCH BUILT IN A WAREHOUSE

CENTRAL BAPTIST CHURCH
Milwaukee, Wisconsin
JAMES MASTIN, *Pastor*

The growth of Central Baptist Church reflects the growth of a man. The embryonic desires that built the church were planted and grew in south Florida. Later, these desires were watered under the preaching of Jack Hyles; and finally, in February 1970, the new congregation was given life.

James Mastin was reared in the First Baptist Church of Miami, Florida, until he was 12 years old. Then he began attending the New Testament Baptist Church when it had only eighty members. Al Janney had started the infant congregation six months prior to that time. As a teenager, James Mastin confesses, "I saw a pioneering spirit and soul-winning zeal that rubbed off on me." The success at the New Testament church made an indelible, subconscious impression that ultimately motivated Mastin to found the Central Baptist Church in Milwaukee.

Mastin had been saved at age ten during a giant Rally Day Sunday School assembly. As the congregation stood to sing an invitational hymn, his Sunday School teacher asked, "Jim, do you need to get saved?" The boy answered, "Yes." Looking around the auditorium at his friends, he added, "But not now."

"Can I pray for you?" the gray-headed Sunday School teacher asked.

"Go ahead," the boy replied.

So the teacher lifted his voice and began praying aloud for the salvation of Jim Mastin, who later replied, "I was so embarrassed, I went forward and accepted Jesus Christ as my Saviour." Mastin has never doubted receiving eternal life and today has no tolerance for those who criticize his church for putting pressure on people to get saved.

Verle Ackerman, Youth and Music Director at New Testament Church, made a direct impact on young Jim, who began teaching Sunday School at age 15 and working as part-time janitor. He rode his bicycle to the church and spent all of his free time there. A new Baptist Bible Fellowship Church was started in Ft. Lauderdale and its excitement spilled over into young Jim Mastin's life. He talked with Ackerman concerning a call to full-time ministry. Ackerman, who has sent many young men off to Bible college, carefully explained the nature of a full-time call into God's service. Finally Ackerman advised, "Don't do something you won't enjoy. The ministry should be the most enjoyable thing in life." Young Mastin wanted to serve God more than anything in life and, two months later, went forward to surrender for the ministry.

After Mastin graduated from Baptist Bible College, Springfield, Missouri, he wanted to start a church in Columbia, South Carolina. However, realizing his youth, he went to work for New Testament Baptist Church, Miami. Mastin managed the bookstore, worked in the bus ministry, taught an adult class and was a substitute teacher in the Christian Grade School. When his best friend, Verle Ackerman, became pastor of the First Baptist Church in West Hollywood, Florida, Mastin was called as Associate Pastor in 1967 when Sunday School attendance averaged 500. He stayed until attendance reached 1,200 in 1969.

"I had always wanted to pastor a church," testified Mastin. "When I went to Jack Hyles' Pastors' School in 1969 the burden became so unbearable I could do nothing but look for a place to start a church."

Jim Mastin moved to Hammond, Indiana for six months in 1969, preparing for a move into the pastorate. Though he worked weekdays as an assistant manager for Kroger's grocery, he learned all he could from Jack Hyles. Throughout this time, Mastin faithfully served in the church.

Taking his wife with him, Mastin visited every major church within 300 miles of Chicago. "The book *The Ten Largest Sunday*

Schools made a substantial impact on my thinking and I visited six of these churches during that six months," the young pastor testified.

Having made up his mind to return to Florida, Mastin again studied his map, stating, "I don't want to miss anything." Realizing they had been in every major city but Milwaukee, early one Sunday the Mastins drove up to the Wisconsin city, arriving at nine o'clock to visit a fundamental church. No one was at the building, so they drove around the city until 9:45. Still, no one was there. Five minutes before Sunday School began, only three cars were present. Mastin was so disgusted he refused to go in. The young couple attended another Baptist church, but no invitation for salvation was given that morning. "This can't be the best church in Milwaukee," Mastin thought, though he had been told it was the largest in the city. The following week, he visited a Conservative Baptist church; again, he found little evangelistic outreach.

Getting a list of Milwaukee churches from the Chamber of Commerce, Mastin surveyed the churches and found that no other conservative church had an auditorium that would appear to seat more than 200 people. "I thought that was impossible in a city of 1,500,000." He didn't realize it, but God was putting a burden upon his heart for Milwaukee. The following day at Kroger's, a Christian truck driver told Mastin he knew just the man to supply information about Milwaukee, Grant Rice. Rice had grown up in Milwaukee and, as the two men prayed together, God impressed Mastin to start a church. When Ackerman was phoned about the project, he said, "Go ahead."

Without doing any door-to-door canvassing in the city, Mastin rented a flat on December 19, 1969, then took off for Miami for a Christmas vacation. The West Hollywood Church had supplied Mastin's car; now they bought him a van which they knew would be more useful in starting a church.

Mastin sold his house, packed a U-Haul trailer and arrived in Milwaukee during a particularly cold January. The temperature was 78° when they left Miami and 12° below when they arrived in Milwaukee. Grant Rice helped him unload their trailer, remarking, "You're either called or crazy."

Still without a meeting place or a name, Mastin began visiting house to house. The biting winds off Lake Michigan kept reminding him of the warm Miami winters. He'd leave his car heater running, visit the length of the block and run back to thaw out. "No one would invite me in," the young preacher confesses. He knocked on 200 doors before Mrs. Liebner let him come in to thaw out. "I never got discouraged, but I sure got cold," the witty young pastor recalled.

Mastin looked at a map, indicating the church ought to be as close as possible to I-94 and I-894, which he calls "the crossroads of Wisconsin." Since this was the central part of the city, he wanted to name his church Central Baptist Church. When God finally gave them a building, it was only a mile from his original location.

James Mastin and his wife visited the Greendale Baptist Church their first week in Wisconsin. When he asked the pastor for prospects on the other side of town where he thought of building a church, the pastor didn't have any. Finally the other preacher remembered, "John Jorgensen used to come, but quit. His parents are in the phone book." When Mastin visited Jorgensen, he found 30 adults meeting in his home on Sunday afternoon to listen to anti-communist tapes.

"If we started a church, would you come?" the unrelenting Mastin asked. Jorgensen answered yes and also supplied the names of 20 families for prospects, although none ever attended. Also Jorgensen remembered trying to sell insurance to a man who had a Bible on his coffee table. When Mastin visited the Keith Knapp family, they agreed to attend.

Still a preacher without a congregation, Mastin tried in vain to rent every possible place for services: civic clubs, banks, funeral homes, and service clubs. Finally the YMCA rented them an 18 x 20 room at $24.50 per week, but the congregation couldn't get into the building until 9:30 A.M. and had to leave at 9:30 in the evening.

Mastin advertised in the local paper that a new church was starting in Milwaukee. Thirteen attended the first service on February 15, 1970. Mastin taught the nine adults in Sunday School; his wife taught the three children. The YMCA wouldn't let them use the other rooms, even though they were empty, so they put a crib in the coat room for the nursery. "When the handful of people got ready to sing, they didn't know a hymn, not one," stated Mastin. His wife played the piano, then took the children to the coat room for children's church. Following the sermon, she came back into the auditorium, turned the children over to some adults, and played for the invitation.

The three messages the first Sunday included: (1) the belief of a church, (2) the goal of a church, and (3) the stand of a church. Fourteen returned for the evening service. Though Mastin persisted, no one was saved during the first six weeks. On Easter 1970, Mr. and Mrs. Keith Knapp brought a sister and brother who were both saved.

Grant Rice preached the organizational service. There were 40 present; 20 became charter members. The following Sunday, five submitted to New Testament baptism in a swimming pool. "We couldn't baptize before this because we were not a church," Mastin stated. Grant Rice gave the church its first printing press, and the Sunday School began to grow. They rented a larger room (28' x 40') at the YMCA for $35.50 a week, keeping the original smaller room. Since they could add to their Sunday School, they bought three buses and began reaching children. Mrs. Mastin once taught 83 juniors in a room 20' x 20'.

The church rented another room 28' x 60' in November, 1971. Then they were able to build a platform and choir loft, making the room look like a church. Sunday School attendance reached 296 on the second anniversary. The "Y" moved to a new building, and Central Baptist Church was then able to rent 5,000 square feet in the old facility for $250.00 a month. Mastin added six buses and attendance reached 476.

The building was always a problem, but not a deterrent to growth. In the early days, a "Y" employee was to be there at 9:30 to open the doors, but on some mornings he didn't arrive until almost 10:00 A.M. Visitors had to stand out in the snow. Mastin didn't know it at first, but six churches had been started in the YMCA. Four had gone out of existence. After the congregation proved themselves, Mastin was given a key to the front door; but still there were problems. On Saturday nights there were dances and he couldn't get in until midnight to clean, scrub, put up chairs, construct a portable platform and put down carpet. Mastin indicated, "People think the YMCA is Christian, but we have cleaned out piles of beer cans and swept cigarette butts off

This modern auditorium was renovated from
a rough warehouse

Pastor James Mastin

Congregation of Central Baptist Church

the dance floor." Also, he had to move out judo pads, gym equipment and set up classrooms for Sunday School. Many mornings Mastin didn't get to bed until 3:00 A.M. The only sign allowed for the church was a small portable A-frame on the sidewalk. It could be used only on Sunday.

One Sunday there were 19 saved. Mastin announced to the congregation, "You see what we can do; we can do more if we had another bus, and one is available." A visitor was so impressed with the appeal that he asked Mastin on the way out how much the bus would cost. When the young preacher said $1,000, the visitor said, "I'll buy it."

Mastin had led another couple to the Lord and they, too, had bought a bus. On September 23, 1971, as they were preparing the building for a special program, a man gave Mastin an envelope. This was about 1:45 Sunday morning. Thinking it was a birthday card, he waited until he started home at 3:30 A.M. to open it. Inside was $1,000 for a bus!

Today, approximately 60 percent of the Sunday School students ride buses that are manned by 30 workers. The diamond green paint job was chosen because of the mud and snow in Milwaukee. "We don't have to wash them so often," Mastin explained.

Mastin noted that when he came to Milwaukee, not one church operated a Sunday morning bus ministry, though some churches owned buses for youth work. Several churches have phoned to ask him to help them get a bus ministry started. Today there are 60 buses in the city.

Mastin believes his radio ministry helped build the church. In September 1971, he called the program *Let's Talk About Jesus*. He simply chatted with the listeners about the progress of the church. Later, the name was changed as Mastin began to perceive that people in the area are extremely conservative. He adopted the more dignified name, *Wisconsin's Gospel Hour*. Even today, a family will attend all services for three to six months before becoming members. Some who have accepted the Lord will even go soul-winning before joining. Mastin notes that they hang onto their original church membership and are slow to leave; but once they make the break, they are faithful and stable, giving the young church a stability that many older churches have not experienced.

The young congregation set a goal of 500 saved during the summer of 1972. Eight Vacation Bible Schools were planned at the old YMCA. Each week, children were bused from a different geographical location. The number actually saved was 857 that summer!

The YMCA gave Mastin a 30-day notice to move on December 1, 1972. He had looked for property for three years. The only suitable acreage was ten miles out in the suburbs, and Mastin didn't want a suburban ministry. "I wanted to be where the people were." He made over 750 contacts for property that month, with anyone who had real estate for sale. A first-class letter telling of their plight was sent to every realtor. There was a flurry of response, but nothing usable opened up.

"I don't know where we will meet next week," Mastin announced to his church on December 31, 1972. "I was embarrassed not to be able to find property," the young preacher testified. "I was their leader and I had failed." He was out until midnight, driving around looking for property, using a flashlight to examine anything available.

"You'll be informed where we'll meet next week," he told the people, not knowing himself where it would be. Twenty-two people joined the church that morning. Mastin told them, "You're crazy, joining a church that doesn't know where it will meet."

Mr. and Mrs. Schwendler phoned their landlord and got permission for prayer meeting to be held in the empty apartment downstairs from their flat. People *crammed* in the prayer meeting; Mastin still couldn't tell them where they would meet on Sunday.

At noon on Friday, a realtor called back indicating he had a furniture warehouse that was "nothing more than a barn" which could be used temporarily.

The building on South 81st Street was to have been a bowling alley and stores, with apartments upstairs. Built in 1927, the Depression caught it while under construction and the investors ran out of money. They had opened the street side to stores, but most recently it had been used as a furniture warehouse.

Just how inappropriate the warehouse was for a church is impossible to describe. The floor in the rear was poured rough concrete. Voices bounced off the four concrete walls and echoed off the dry wall ceiling, making it impossible to preach. The floor for the front section was of rough tongue-and-groove boards. There was only one small restroom, barely large enough for a commode. Someone remarked it was "so small a person had to back in to use it." A small, undersized door opened to the street but swung the wrong way. There were no fire exits. Four small space heaters suspended from the ceiling could only warm the building to 60 degrees in the frigid Wisconsin winters. The people had to sit bundled in their coats during the service.

The owners wanted $1,000 a month when Mastin asked about renting it. They were more interested in selling it for $135,000.

"I could tell you more about purchasing it if you would let us use it for a month." Mastin offered them $250 rent, but they let him use it free since he was considering the purchase.

A phone committee had been set up to inform the congregation where church would meet that first Sunday in January, 1973. Mastin called a lady and she called ten others, who in turn contacted everyone else.

Mastin had bought 200 chairs in Chicago to use, along with the 150 they had at the YMCA. The members worked feverishly all Saturday—cleaning, scrubbing, constructing a platform and covering it with carpet. A Christian music store loaned them a public address system. Mastin smiled in retrospect. "The greatest miracle in my life was getting that building and occupying it in one day."

Verle Ackerman preached in the warehouse/auditorium the following month, February, 1973. Attendance reached 417. When asked about the advisability of using the building permanently, Ackerman answered, "Sure, if you've got a good imagination." The men of the church said they couldn't visualize the warehouse as a permanent home, but Mastin began to picture how the building could be used as a church. He drew a floor plan and assigned space allocations. The men of the church said, "Go ahead." Mastin indicated no one had a good opinion about the building.

The owners of the building had been stuck with a white elephant warehouse in a trade and were trying to get $135,000. Mastin worked out some sketches with their architect and asked the owners to remodel the building and sell it to him as a package deal. After much dickering with the company, they supplied the architect and contractor, doing $90,000 worth of remodeling, constructing a main auditorium, a vestibule, nursery, the required exits, bringing the building up to city code. The outside entrances to the basement were sealed and two inside stairways constructed. Whereas the owners had asked $135,000 for the building, Mastin paid $150,000 for the completed project. The owners claimed they lost money, but in the providence of God, a church was being built in Central Milwaukee.

Mastin raised $50,000 immediately by issuing open notes to his congregation. More importantly, the congregation didn't have to pay rent for the next eleven months, giving them time to establish a financial basis for the new obligation.

Before construction started, the city inspectors came by and said it was illegal for the church to use the building. "You can't put us in the street," Mastin reasoned. He testifies that the city was reasonable. The inspectors didn't come back until the remodeling had begun.

Church services were difficult to carry on during construction. Even though they dusted ten minutes before service, the space heaters kicked up sawdust, spreading a fine talcum over the entire congregation. When the one commode was flushed, it could be heard all over the auditorium. The old fluorescent light would blink when kids stomped on the floor in the second-story Sunday School facilities. Yet, Mastin affirms, adversity strengthened the congregation. People kept coming, and each week the building conditions got better. Good families became members and the congregation grew by 150 during the refurbishing process.

The new building was dedicated April 29, 1973. Sunday School attendance had reached 725. The attorneys, plumbers, carpenters and all who had helped on the building were invited for a great victory celebration. Dr. William Dowell spoke at the 10 A.M. hour and Mastin spoke at 11 A.M.; over 40 were saved that day.

During the summer of 1973, Sunday School hit a slump. Mastin indicated he was not ready for it. The previous summer the church had held eight VBS's and attendance had soared. The church had given all of its energies to occupy the new building. Attendance dipped to 300 in Sunday School during the summer of 1973. Despite the drop in attendance among kids, adult attendance grew during the summer. The fall drive began with 683, reaching a high of 862 on December 9, 1973. Sunday School averaged 615 for the 1973 fall.

During the church's first year, 62 people walked the aisle, which Mastin considered a great victory. Yet in their third year, 75 walked the aisle in a single service. A total of 1,129 people made professions in 1973, and 218 were baptized from May to December.

Mastin indicated three men made a great impression on his life. First, Jack Hyles taught him how to be a leader. Today, he preaches hard like Jack Hyles, even though he had preached earlier in his life. Verle Ackerman taught him the necessity of details and organization. Al Janney gave him a pioneering spirit. Today Mastin testifies, "If it were not for these three men, Central Baptist Church wouldn't be in Milwaukee." He notes that almost every church in Milwaukee is run by committees (deacons) and Hyles taught him how to lead a church. As a result of this, Central Baptist Church has had few problems in its direction of administration. Mastin indicates, "It would have been impossible to build a church in Milwaukee on deacon-controlled leadership."

From the very beginning Mastin told his people that "God uses a leader in every church and God will do it here." Each month he passes out a complete financial statement and there have been no financial problems in the church. Mastin waited almost three years before he elected deacons. Today, he testifies, "Our people wouldn't have it any other way. Before deacons could be elected, they had to be qualified, practicing soul-winners, separated from worldly activities."

Many think that strong pastoral leadership is built on naïve or weak Christians. "Not so," according to Mastin. He indicated that the stable, conservative people of Milwaukee respond more to a strong pastor than to a committee. Yet Mastin realized that the average pastor can't exercise strong leadership as he does, explaining, "As long as we have unsaved walking the aisle every Sunday, the congregation will follow my leadership." He noticed that when a church is a social club, "the people want to control it." He concluded, "As long as we stir the baptismal waters each week, our people will respond to pastoral leadership."

The church has taken a strong stand on separation from worldly practices. "We are the only church in the city to preach against short skirts, long hair, and women wearing slacks." He feels that God blesses purity, hence he preaches hard against sin.

Auditorium of Central Baptist Church in furniture warehouse
before new pews were added

CHAPTER THREE

A CHURCH BUILT WITH DIGNITY

FAIRFAX BAPTIST TEMPLE
Fairfax, Virginia
BUD CALVERT, *Pastor*

Some churches seem to be founded with dignity, like the baby born with a silver spoon in his mouth and blue blood coursing through his veins. The Fairfax Baptist Temple has a stamp of majesty upon its infant profile. Located in a suburb of Washington, D.C., it ministers in the environment of one of the most influential cities in the world. Its congregation is not rich, nor are they poor. The standards for church workers demand purity as though announcing, "Only the qualified serve here; mediocrity is insufficient." The pastor and founder, Bud Calvert, is dignified yet friendly; he is obviously educated, yet realizes the potential of his success is the power of God that only flows through yielded human vessels.

Bud Calvert was born in Arlington, Virginia, October 1943, and lived there all of his life. At age 17, he joined the Army and was shipped overseas. While he was in Italy, his mother sent him a Bible along with Christian books and literature.

After returning home, he was searching for answers to life and visited a Baptist church in Arlington one Sunday morning. That evening, he returned. The young adults were planning a camp and when Bud realized the girl at the piano was going, he decided to join the group.

On Saturday evening, June 4, 1965, sitting around a campfire, many people were sharing their testimonies; some were crying. "These were people I respected," confessed Calvert, "Yet, they

27

Pastor Bud Calvert

were not ashamed to show their love for Christ." Sitting there that evening, he accepted the Lord. No one dealt with him from the Scripture; it was just a definite decision to give his life to God. Calvert got up and gave a testimony—the first time in his life he ever remembered crying for a spiritual reason.

Almost immediately, he had a burden to return to Arlington and begin a church. Now Calvert looks back and comments, "Since it took so long to reach me, I knew the area needed the gospel." Also, he *knew* God was calling him to the area because "my heart was here." (Rom. 10:1-4). Calvert suggests several practical advantages for a young man pastoring a church in his home: he knows the area well, saving perhaps a year getting adjusted to the business community; he can find his way around; he is known by and knows the people; he has the "feel" of the community.

Calvert believes he received his spiritual gift of "pastor-teacher" (Eph. 4:11) shortly after his salvation. He indicates, "God gave me a gift for the purpose of establishing a New Testament Baptist Church."

He counsels young men, "Make sure you understand and identify your calling and gift from God. Do not hide under the canopy of the term, 'full-time Christian service'." He counsels a young man to know exactly his desires for the ministry and to train accordingly. Calvert feels a burden upon his life, "Woe is unto me if I preach not the gospel." (I Cor. 9:16).

Bud Calvert attended Bob Jones University for four years. After graduation, during the summer of 1970, he met Grant Rice in Chicago, Illinois. Rice encouraged him to begin a church. Calvert brought his tape recorder along and met Rice at the Oak Forest Baptist Temple. The experienced Rice asked, "Did God call you to preach?" Calvert said, Yes."

"Did God call you to start a church?" Once again, Calvert answered, "Yes."

"Why wait?"

"I told my wife we were going to start a church even though I was scared," Calvert said. He also confessed he did not have an idea of how to begin. Calvert wrote out a list of questions and took along his tape recorder for the next session where Rice answered every question and encouraged, "You can do it."

Shortly before Calvert came to northern Virginia, another pastor in the area asked him to be his assistant. Calvert responded, "God did not call me to be an assistant, but to start a church." This invitation by another church compelled Calvert to start a church *immediately*.

He had obligated his summer to travel with the college ensemble. In Michigan, he met a lady who startled him by saying, "I was at your mother's funeral and heard you preach." The lady continued, "I've been praying for years for someone to start a church in northern Virginia." Calvert never saw the lady again.

Next, he counseled with several of the teachers at college. They all encouraged him to start the church immediately.

As he drove through the southern suburb of Washington, D.C., Bud found that Arlington, Virginia, was already developed. So he looked into other communities. He called the Chamber of Commerce and asked what community had the greatest potential of growth. Next, he talked to the police to determine an area.

As he began to look at property, he found that much of it was exorbitant in price. One land developer wanted one million dollars an acre. Since land was cheaper and the community was being developed in Fairfax, he eventually settled there. But Calvert wanted to get away from the community church concept. He announced, "The church is only the focal place; we will reach into Arlington and other nearby areas by Sunday School bus." He announced to his infant congregation, "A church building is only a centralized place to reach northern Virginia."

The Calverts had a two-bedroom apartment on the second floor in Annandale, Virginia. They held their first Bible study there in October 1970, on a Tuesday night. He chose Tuesday because there was no church meeting then. Immediately he realized a Bible study wasn't the way to begin a church in this area. He looks back and confesses that a Bible study group would have been an easy crutch, but would slow down the progress of the church. He commented about a Bible study: "People have no responsibility to the preacher, to others in the group or the future." As a result, he could see only slow growth in the Bible study.

Today, he counsels a young preacher, "Jump in and get started." He notes the pressure will make both the preacher and the Sunday School teachers work harder. "If we jump off the dock, we have to swim. Begin the church immediately, and you will have to exhibit more faith and will become a church sooner. I never considered a Bible study as a stepping stone to a church. Many men who want to start a church, work for a living and begin a Bible study, hoping it will get off the ground. When enough finances come in, the pastor goes on full time." Calvert quotes the Scripture, "They which preach the gospel should live of the gospel" (I Cor. 9:14). Then he responds, "I determined to start a church and let it support me." This was his positive mental action being worked out in life.

There was a total of six in that first service in his apartment: the three Calverts, Dave and Margaret Abbey and their little boy. The church met for three weeks in the apartment, and Bud signed a year's contract to rent West Springfield High School at $25 a week. There were 39 in attendance for Sunday School on October 25, 1970. To get that crowd, Bud spent hours knocking on doors, then advertised in the newspaper and radio with money that a new convert had given to him. (Bud had led an Army friend to the Lord who gave him $300 to start the church.) For that first service, Bud

invited every relative he had within a 100-mile radius and humorously chided them, "Be there, or else."

In keeping with his usual thoroughness, Calvert already had a
constitution drawn up and a budget prepared. He knew he could
live on $85 a week and told the church that first Sunday how much
salary they needed. For that first offering, the Calverts put in $100
(money he and his wife had been saving) to insure himself a salary.
Calvert had determined before God that he would work as hard
as possible as a full-time preacher, trusting God to provide the
financial means.

Rather than use unqualified teachers, Calvert started with the
principle that he would teach every group in Sunday School until
God gave him qualified, separated, soul-winning teachers. At first,
his wife, Mary, took the nursery and the small kids; he taught the
others. Within weeks, Dave and Margaret Abbey became teachers.
The Sunday School was divided into departments.

From the very beginning, the church had high standards of
leadership. Calvert maintains that to use "just anybody" to get the
job done would have hurt his growth. Rather, he feels God has
honored his standards and brought people to his church who want
a biblical position of separation. All workers agree to the standards
regarding teaching responsibilities, which include personal habits
and dress: "I will maintain clean habits of life and modesty (knee-
length dresses for women and no long hair for men) in my
personal appearance as a leader of this church. I will not participate in worldly amusements or habits such as dancing, theater
going, the use of tobacco or alcoholic beverages or any other
amusements or habits that may be contrary to the standards of this
church and the Word of God."

In the early days, Calvert set a visitation policy of going out
Tuesday, Thursday and Friday evenings and again on Saturday,
taking a different man with him to train him in soul-winning. Today, he believes the growth of the church is a result of dedicated
soul-winners.

The church was organized two months later on December 6,
with 23 charter members. Grant Rice preached at the organizational
meeting.

Almost immediately, the church began looking for property; they
needed a focal point to tie the church together. Calvert contacted

a Christian realtor to help look for four or five acres. They found one plot at $20,000 an acre on a back road, but it was unacceptable. The present location of five acres was tied up in the courts.

As soon as Calvert found the property, he called for a meeting of all of the men of the church. They agreed to purchase the property but there was one hitch—they didn't have any money! Calvert noted, "We needed a miracle to show our people that the God we served was great and that he would supply our needs."

Calvert knew he had to act fast. He submitted a bid of $50,000, or $10,000 an acre. The property was awarded to the church on February 1, 1971. Calvert had searched for finances for a down payment. The young congregation had no cash assets. He planned to ask several people to loan him $4,000 or $5,000 down. Then, he planned to approach a bank with his down payment and ask for a loan. A Christian couple loaned him $5,000, then phoned him back, "Why don't you let us lend you the total $50,000 at six per cent?"

The young congregation had two miracles: first, the property; second, the loan. Calvert exclaimed, "That did something for me and the church." As soon as the church bought the five acres for $50,000, a developer offered to buy one back acre for $40,000, leaving them four acres. Although they didn't sell it, this verified in Calvert's mind that God had given them the right property.

After the church bought this property, 50 acres became available six miles away. But the price was high and the location off the main thoroughfare. Calvert phoned the author about the choice. I told him, "Don't mortgage the present on future expansion." The young congregation would have had property, but could not have built. I felt it was better to construct a building and expand immediately on the five acres rather than buy a larger acreage and postpone building. Growth could also have been curtailed.

The church began giving to foreign missions during its first weeks of meetings. They set aside money for foreign missions. When a missionary visited them in its third month of existence, they had a check waiting to give him.

In the summer of 1971, Calvert felt God wanted him to start a bus ministry so he asked for volunteers. No one volunteered. Finally, Jim Histand indicated willingness to start a route. In July, they started a bus route without a bus, bringing children to church by cars. Finally, someone donated $1,000 to purchase a bus and riders began coming to the church. Someone else donated $1,000 for a second bus.

Walt and Georgia Beach moved to the area from Forrest Hills Baptist Church, Decatur, Georgia and visited several independent Baptist churches in the area. However, they were looking for a congregation with the same evangelistic zeal that they had back in Decatur, Georgia. Walt saw a bus in the shopping center and phoned around, but couldn't find the church. Even the Fire Department didn't know about its existence. Walt kept seeing the buses, finally getting the phone number and visiting the church at West Springfield High School. Today, Walt is as excited about this church as his previous one and has been elected as a deacon.

Fairfax County has 500,000 people and an average income of $18,200 per family. There are no poor sections within miles of the church; therefore, it does not bus children from the ghettos or inner cities. The church is flanked by two subdivisions with homes in the $60,000 bracket. Jim Histand, a former Air Force Captain, had a high of 101 on his bus, astounding when you consider the fact that the riders come from a middle-class area.

The church reached an attendance of 139 on its first anniversary. That Sunday morning, an architect's rendering of a proposed $200,000 building was revealed to the congregation. Although the congregation was not able to start building for another year, the picture gave stability and hope to the young congregation. It built a sense of mission in the community.

The church is now averaging more than 500 in Sunday School with a high attendance of 814 and a weekly offering of $1,800. The congregation owns ten buses, all bought by special gifts from the people. The church has a full-time Assistant Pastor, a part-time Youth Director and a full-time secretary.

Every morning, a 15-minute live radio broadcast comes from the pastor's office designed to share the church with those in the community. It holds up soul-winning and the goals of Fairfax Baptist Temple. Also, the church publishes a monthly newsletter that goes to all of those who have visited the Fairfax Baptist Temple.

The church plans to begin building its second building in 1975 at the cost of $500,000. They are shooting for 1,004 in Sunday

Fairfax Baptist Temple

School on the fourth anniversary and Calvert hopes that by 1976 they can start a Christian day school.

"I was not that baptistic in the beginning of the church, but read and studied all I could find on the local church." Today Calvert confesses, "I am more baptistic because of my love for the local church and conviction that it is God's primary instrument." Calvert indicates, "It was difficult for me to understand pastoral leadership; this was a whole new concept." He appreciates Dr. Jack Hyles showing him the dignity of the pastorate. He indicates he has been influenced by *The Ten Largest Sunday Schools* and *America's Fastest Growing Churches,* books written about successful churches by the author. Calvert learned from these examples how to build a great church.

There has been no doubt about Bud's pastoral leadership from the beginning. He moderates the deacons' meetings, following no set pattern. They just accomplish the business at hand. The men respect him greatly as he looks to them for advice.

Bud Calvert is an immaculately dressed preacher. Whatever he does is first class. He desires no compromise in standards or production. When someone noted to Calvert, "You couldn't have started a church in a dance hall or an empty store," he smiled agreement.

As you walk through the building, it is impeccably clean. Just like his office, everything is in place. Of the church auditoriums among the young churches of this book, this building has a stamp of elegance; quality construction is evident everywhere.

Calvert indicates a young pastor must keep a positive attitude, trying to find ways to build people up, rather than emphasizing the negative to beat them down. He tells other young preachers that *they* must get a positive attitude established in their mind before they can establish a positive attitude in the minds of the people.

Calvert is characterized as a doctrinal preacher, even though he emphasizes salvation every Sunday. One man commented that Calvert's sermons were straight to the point. "You don't have to go home and think about it." Calvert has chosen as his life-preaching verse I Corinthians 2:4 which says, "And my speech and my preaching was not with enticing words of man's wisdom, but in demonstration of the Spirit and of power." This is his goal for all of his preaching.

Yet, the church is not like the typical evangelistic-fundamentalist church. People don't visit as strangers and immediately walk the aisle; they recognize that the water is pretty deep. Before a person becomes a member of Fairfax Baptist Temple, he usually realizes the church has high standards of separation. New members are expected to get involved, and most Christians visit a long time before they join. Many don't join at all, but go to an "easy" church.

CHAPTER FOUR

BEGINNING A CHURCH IN HIS HOME TOWN

CALVARY BIBLE CHURCH
Lincoln, Nebraska
CARL GODWIN, *Pastor*

Carl Godwin graduated from Lincoln (Nebraska) High School in 1965, and, because he felt called to full-time Christian service, entered Bethany Nazarene College, Oklahoma, receiving B.A. and M.A. degrees. During his last year in college he read *The Ten Largest Sunday Schools and What Makes Them Grow* by the author. This book instigated a life-changing experience. Godwin asked approval from his mentor to interview pastors from these large churches as a thesis for his master's degree, but was turned down. The thesis advisor rationalized, "That 1971 topic will not make a contribution to knowledge."

During the spring, I lectured at the college on trends among the large churches. After graduation, Godwin decided to spend a year studying some of the world's largest and fastest-growing churches. He moved to Hammond, Indiana and worked in a steel mill. For seven months, he analyzed the First Baptist Church of Hammond, trying to learn how Jack Hyles built the world's largest Sunday School.

Halfway through the year, he moved to Lynchburg, Virginia, and served on the staff of Thomas Road Baptist Church, studying Jerry Falwell's concept of saturation evangelism. He testified, "Hyles taught me how to build a church, but Jerry challenged me to do it. There is something infectious about Thomas Road that makes a man want to build a church."

37

Pastor Carl Godwin

While living in Lynchburg, he became a close friend of the author, having previously known him only through his books and lectures. As the author went to weekend speaking appointments, Godwin drove the car, giving the author opportunity to study, dictate letters or catch up on lost sleep. During every opportunity, young Godwin "picked my brains" to learn everything I knew about building a large church.

During these trips to fast-growing churches (I was doing a series for *The Sword Of The Lord* on fast-growing churches), God put a burden on Godwin's heart to return home to Lincoln and found a New Testament church. Even before going home, he chose the name "Calvary Bible Church" and began praying for God's blessing upon the work.

Godwin stopped by the computer room of the Thomas Road Baptist Church to get a list of all the Christians in Lincoln who had written to the Old Time Gospel Hour, a telecast of the church's Sunday morning service. He got over 100 names and began compiling a mailing of prospects, even before arriving in Lincoln.

Within the first few days in Lincoln, he located an auditorium at the Christian Record Braille Foundation and arranged to rent it for $20.00 a week, beginning July 1, 1973. He had three weeks in Lincoln to get ready for his first service. "I didn't realize how much detail there was to getting a church started," the young preacher stated. Envelopes and letterheads had to be printed, flyers prepared, and a lawyer contacted to incorporate the church as a nonprofit organization. Among other things, he and his wife, Gayle, needed to rent a house. She went to work in a public school system to support the family, while Godwin gave full time to the church.

Godwin got out his high school annual *The Link* and put his old high school buddies on his mailing list. As he began visiting, a former friend, Doug Gregg and his wife, Carolyn, received the Lord.

Godwin's father, treasurer for the local plumbers' union, supplied 70 names of prospects within the city, who also were added to the mailing list. Newcomers to Lincoln were added to the list.

Three thousand flyers announcing "Lincoln's newest church" were distributed on Saturday afternoon, June 31, the day before the first meeting. A copy of the flyer was printed in the local newspaper announcing the new church. The local newspaper also gave news coverage to the young congregation.

Godwin reflected, "I didn't know how many would come our first Sunday," but only 19 arrived for Sunday School, including his relatives and some friends from out of town. He was discouraged. The young preacher admits, "I was down" because of the small crowd. After teaching the lesson, he went to the front door and found a larger crowd waiting; there were 55 for that first morning service. Godwin had forgotten that most of the residents were Lutheran, not trained to come to Sunday School. Fifty-five at a first service may not be a record, but it encouraged a new pastor.

"We had to set up extra chairs that first day," related Godwin. "The crowd was a dream come true." He preached a very simple sermon, "Jesus, a Friend of Sinners." When one family stepped out to confess Christ that first Sunday, Godwin knew that God was going to use him to build a soul-winning church in Lincoln.

Attendance peaked again at 74 on August 18 when the author

visited to speak to the infant congregation. I brought a series of messages on the local church, first defining a church, indicating that if Calvary Bible Church fit the New Testament qualifications, it would (1) accept only members who professed faith in Jesus Christ and have been baptized; (2) hold up the presence of the living Christ in their congregation; (3) place themselves under the discipline of the Scriptures; (4) be organized for evangelism, education, worship, fellowship; (5) administer the ordinances; and (6) exercise spiritual gifts of leadership needed to build a church.

In my second message, I challenged the congregation to carry out the Great Commission and saturate the 170,000 people of Greater Lincoln with the gospel. I described saturation evangelism as "preaching the gospel by every available means to every available person at every available time." Carl Godwin had been telling the people he wanted to reach the city of Lincoln, but when I reinforced his vision, it added credibility to his sermons. I told Godwin when he went to Lincoln that he should have authorities to speak to his people; these men would expand the vision of his people, as well as substantiate his ministry. I reminded him that the people of Lincoln had never heard of a super-aggressive church that wants to reach an entire city. They think in terms of a local neighborhood parish church, the typical American view of Christianity. God's Word teaches us to use every means to reach everyone. So I challenged the congregation to a large vision: 30 buses covering the city, a daily radio broadcast, a weekly telecast, a church newspaper, an organized, trained corps of workers to knock on every door and phone every home with the message of the gospel.

Many of the new Christians had not heard of this type of church, but it was what they wanted. The church accepted the challenge and followed the leadership of Godwin. Their first purchase was a printing press, and the second purchase was a Sunday School bus to bring children to Sunday School.

That first visit, I challenged the congregation to buy 20 acres of ground two or three miles outside the city, while property was cheap, so they could plan for a massive city-wide ministry. "Time is on your side, and within three or four years the city will grow out to you; your church will be the first in the area and new families will visit your services."

At the morning service, I dared the congregation of 61 adults to set four goals: (1) to average 2,000 in Sunday School; (2) to send many young men into the ministry; (3) to support missionaries in a worldwide outreach, and (4) to saturate the city with the gospel. That morning I gave Godwin a check for $200 to begin a building fund, to be used specifically for a down payment on property. Later that week, an attender added $500 to the fund. This fund would encourage a young congregation as well as provide an incentive to get started on the property. A group of people unorganized and without property needed the security of money in the bank and the responsibility of looking for a future home.

THE ORGANIZATIONAL MEETING

The congregation of Calvary Bible Church met for the first 13 weeks without organizing into a local church. Carl Godwin preached each Sunday and visited during the week, doing all those things necessary to bring a New Testament Church into existence. The Sunday School and morning service resembled a local church; however, Godwin was not able to give a gospel invitation for people to come forward and join the church because there was no membership yet. Also, he could not baptize new converts nor serve the Lord's table. Church ordinances can only be administered by a local church. Not every group of Christians that conducts religious services is a New Testament church, even though they go by the generic title *church*. A congregation must meet the New Testament requirements. The organizational meeting of a group of people does not make them a New Testament church. An organizational meeting only recognizes the work that God has done in their midst, just as ordination does not make a man more spiritual nor does it call him into the ministry. Ordination is an act by church leaders where "the laying on of hands" is simply man's recognition of God's call into the ministry. After 13 weeks of existence, the members of Calvary Bible Church felt they qualified as a New Testament church and invited me to come and organize them.

First, the church had assembled a number of Christians who sensed the hand of God upon them as sermons were preached and the lost were won to Christ. Second, they enjoyed fellowship with one another and were determined to place themselves under the Word of God. Resisting my suggestion to call themselves a Baptist church, they wanted to be known as a Bible church. Third, they had organized visitation. The bus brought in children who were won to Christ, spreading a zeal for soul-winning. Fourth, there was never a doubt in the people's minds that Carl Godwin was sent by God to build a church; he was their spiritual leader. Therefore, since they had the characteristics of a church, they were ready to be organized.

About 50 people gathered on a Monday evening, September 24, 1973, for the organizational service. The congregation had already been incorporated as a nonprofit organization in the State of Nebraska. This enabled them to receive finances, pay bills, own property and issue tax receipts.

I preached a sermon at the organizational meeting on the responsibilities of members to their church. Since the New Testament church was a group of baptized believers, I challenged them to faith in Jesus Christ and to receive only those into fellowship who had like faith and had been baptized. Since a New Testament church had the presence of Jesus Christ in their midst, I challenged them to allow Christ to shine through their corporate testimony and to use every means possible to hold forth the light of Christ into the city of Lincoln. Since the New Testament church placed itself under the discipline of the Word of God, I challenged them to reverence, believe, obey, and teach the Word of God. Since the New Testament church is organized for evangelism, education, worship and fellowship, I challenged them to give attention to their organization and always to keep soul-winning foremost in their program. Since a New Testament church administers the ordinances of baptism and the Lord's table, I challenged them to baptize all who came to know Jesus Christ and to administer the Lord's table to accomplish its purposes. Since the New Testament church is evidenced by the exercise of spiritual gifts, I challenged the congregation to follow the leadership of their pastor, a gifted man.

At the end of the sermon, I read the doctrinal statement of the church, briefly explaining each of the ten points. (See end of this chapter for Statement.) Then, a printed copy of the preamble to the constitution was distributed. I opened the invitation, "Everyone who wants to become a charter member of this New Testa-

Top:
Bus Workers at Calvary Bible Church

Middle:
Pastor and Mrs. Carl Godwin

Bottom:
Exterior View

ment church, please come forward and take one of the seats in the first three rows."

I told those who came forward they should be a Christian, giving testimony of their living relationship to Jesus Christ. Next, they should be baptized by immersion in water as a confession of their faith. Finally, they had to be in agreement with the doctrine and practice of this church as printed in the constitution and distributed. Several people had their letters in hand from previous church affiliations. Some had not been baptized, but they presented themselves as candidates for both membership and baptism and they expressed willingness to be immersed as soon as the church could arrange a baptismal service.

Eighteen people came forward and seated themselves in the first three rows. They were instructed to sign the preamble, indicating their desire to become a member of this church. After the signed documents were gathered, I stated, "By the authority of Nebraska which has incorporated Calvary Bible Church as a nonprofit organization, and by your declaration to form yourselves into a New Testament church, I declare you are organized as a New Testament church."

I then declared the business meeting open to ratify the name "Calvary Bible Church" and the constitution that had been distributed. I felt it was important for the congregation to approve the name and business procedures. The name had been chosen by Godwin. The constitution had also been written by Godwin but over several weeks, he had discussed each item with the congregation at prayer meeting. The name and constitution were approved. Next, a motion was received to call as its first pastor, Carl Godwin. All over the room hands went up to make the motion and to second it. A unanimous "Amen!" confirmed Godwin as the pastor. Next, a treasurer was elected and the congregation approved the financial records and cash disbursements thus far.

Concerning the election of deacons, I told the people this election was one of the most important for the future of the church; therefore, I urged them to wait for six months. During that time, men with spiritual gifts would emerge into places of lay leadership. Then, under the leadership of the pastor, a board of deacons could be elected by the congregation. Since there were only five men among the charter members, I suggested that the pastor use all five men in the role of deacons without officially electing them, turning to them for advice and direction in making decisions. I pointed out to the charter members that the New Testament teaches pastoral leadership, not a committee-controlled church. Nowhere does the Bible teach that deacons are to make decisions concerning finances and policy; this is a congregational matter. Since deacons are to advise and assist the pastor, all of the men of the church could carry out this function in the early days.

Next, a motion was made to keep charter membership open for 60 days, so that others not present that evening could become charter members.

I challenged the new pastor to faithfully discharge his responsibility, even in discouraging times. Then, I gave him the promise of God and applied it to the congregation: "Faithful is he that calleth you, who also will do it." (I Thess. 5:23). I noted, The promise of God is clear. If God has called this congregation together, he will perform its growth and ministry through pastor and people."

CALVARY BIBLE CHURCH   LINCOLN, NEBRASKA
IN THE YEAR OF OUR LORD, SEPTEMBER 24, 1973
WE, the undersigned, relying on the guidance of the Holy Spirit
and by the signing of our names hereto do agree and covenant
with the Lord Jesus Christ and with one another that we do constitute ourselves as Charter Members of the Calvary Bible Church,
Lincoln, Nebraska.
FURTHER, we, the undersigned, each declare and confess with
our faith wholly in the Lord Jesus Christ for salvation by the experience of the new birth that we have been Scripturally baptized
and therefore are qualified to become Charter Members.
ALSO, we, the undersigned, do believe in those great distinctive
principles for which born again Christians have ever stood, namely:

1. The pre-eminence of Christ as our Divine Lord and
   Master
2. The supreme authority of the Bible and its sufficiency as
   our only rule of faith and practice
3. The right of private interpretation and the competency of
   the individual soul in direct approach to God
4. The absolute separation of Church and State
5. The regenerate church membership
6. The beautiful symbolic ordinance of believer's baptism
   and the Lord's Supper in obedience to the command of
   Christ
7. The complete independence of the local church and its
   interdependence in associated fellowship with other
   churches
8. The solemn obligation of majority rule, guaranteeing equal
   rights to all and special privileges to none
9. A world-wide program of missionary fervor and evangelism in obedience to the final command of the Lord Jesus
   Christ
10. The personal, imminent, pre-millennial return of the Lord
    Jesus Christ.

AND, we, the undersigned, accept the doctrines of the Articles of
Faith included herein; and, accept the duties of the Church Covenant included herein; we assemble ourselves together as the Calvary Bible Church, and adopt for our plan of outreach, govern-
ment, and service the By-Laws included herein.

COVENANT

As a bond of unity among us Calvary Bible Church accepts for its members the following covenant.

Having been led by the Holy Spirit to receive the Lord Jesus Christ as our Saviour and on profession of our faith in Him, having been baptized in the name of the Father, and of the Son, and of the Holy Spirit, we do now most solemnly and joyfully enter into covenant with one another as one body in Christ.

We promise that we will watch over and counsel one another in the spirit of brotherly love, that we will remember one another in our prayers, and that we will aid each other in sickness and distress.

We further agree, by the aid of the Holy Spirit, to walk together in Christian love; to strive for the advancement of this church in knowledge, holiness, and comfort; to promote its prosperity and spirituality; to sustain its worship, ordinances, discipline, and doctrines; to give it a sacred pre-eminence over all institutions of human origin; and to contribute cheerfully and regularly to the support of the ministry, the expenses of the church, the relief of the poor, and the spread of the Gospel through all nations.

We further covenant to maintain family and private devotion; to religiously educate our children; to seek the salvation of our kindred and acquaintances; to live carefully in this present world; to be just in our dealings, faithful in our engagements, and exemplary in our deportment; to avoid all tattling, backbiting, and excessive anger; to abstain from everything that will cause our brother to stumble or that will bring reproach upon the cause of Christ; and to strive to grow in the grace and knowledge of our Lord and Saviour, that amidst evil and good report we will humbly and earnestly seek to live to the honor and glory of Him who loved us and gave Himself for us.

We moreover engage that when we remove from this place we will, as soon as possible, unite with some other church where we can carry out the spirit of this covenant and the principles of God's Word.

CHAPTER FIVE

A GREAT FIRST ANNIVERSARY

CANYON CREEK BAPTIST CHURCH
Richardson, Texas
PERRY PURTLE, *Pastor*

One of the largest first anniversary celebrations for a church was held September 17, 1973, at Canyon Creek Baptist Church, Richardson, Texas, when 1,103 gathered to celebrate the church's first birthday. Over twelve hundred were present for the morning service. Six months before the anniversary, Dr. Perry Purtle, pastor, distributed to each member a label "I Love 1,000," planning for a record-shattering crowd. The day before the anniversary, he sent the people into every home in the neighborhood, announcing, "Come and be part of history in the making." The growth of the church in its first year made their claim credible, creating community-wide interest. Dr. Purtle made extensive plans to reach 1,000, and the people were ready to follow his leadership. Not a member doubted they would reach the goal.

But more than a large crowd, the one-year-old infant had maturity and stability on its first birthday: assets were valued at a half-million dollars; attendance was running over 400; 222 people were baptized in the first year, and membership had reached 379. Offerings reached $75,000 for the first year and the people realistically thought, "We can build the greatest church since Pentecost." It remains to be seen whether they can, but no one at that exciting first anniversary would tell them otherwise.

The church met in a rented elementary school during its first year. When Purtle planned the big anniversary, they recognized there was not enough room or chairs in the school to accommodate

48

the anticipated crowd. The church owned 7.3 acres and had the outside shell of a $200,000 building erected, but the facilities were not ready for an invasion by the masses. A large red-and-white circus tent seating 1,000 was pitched on the building site. According to Dr. Purtle, "I wanted the peopje to get the excitement of being near our half-completed building." But the idea of a tent caused problems. The church is surrounded by $100,000 homes; the prestigious Canyon Creek has one of the highest household income rates in the Greater Dallas area. "Would sophisticated people worship in a tent?" Purtle pondered. Fresh sawdust was strewn, an elaborate stereophonic amplification system was rented and a large carpeted platform was built.

Nineteen members of the Dallas Symphony Orchestra dressed in tuxedos provided musical background for the 36-voice church choir, and the stereophonic melodies of Bill Gaither's music brought a "sweet, sweet spirit" to the meeting. The choir, dressed in blue-and-white print mu-mu robes warmed up like an oratorio choir with the accompaniment of the grand piano and organ. Sophistication was everywhere apparent. But when the congregation joined in singing "Oh, How I Love Jesus," a revival spirit filled the tent.

David Compton is a layman sent by God to the church to direct the music program. He scored the music and arranged the renditions for the occasion, adding a luxurious image to the nostalgic old hymns. Friday night Dave's mother died, but he felt constrained to stay; the funeral was put off until Monday so he could take part in the first anniversary service.

Purtle told those under the tent how he had led a handful of people to the very spot 52 weeks previously, where they prayed and asked God to give them the property. Young Pastor Purtle had driven through the area and found 4.7 acres; he offered $50,000 to a Jewish real estate broker. "$100,000 is the price," the broker had said, unsympathetic with Purtle's vision.

If persistence builds a church, the young pastor was unrelenting. The next week, Purtle went to see him again and upped the offer to $53,000, indicating, "I'll pay closing costs."

"No." The property was reserved for a shopping center. The owner told him an offer had already been made for $75,000. Two weeks later, Purtle visited him again and re-offered $53,000. Deep

Artist's conception of Canyon Creek Baptist Church. Construction of a seven story prayer tower began October 1974.

Pastor Jerry Purtle

Pastor Purtle addresses "First Anniversary" congregation

in his heart he felt God wanted him to build a church on that spot—so much so, that he led his people into the middle of the field after a morning church service and asked God to work a miracle.

The following week, the owner phoned and offered the property to him for $53,000; later, the broker gave the church almost an acre. Two other acres were purchased from another party.

After the price of $53,000 was agreed upon, Purtle was able to borrow $35,000 from a local loan company. They agreed to loan him the money if he could raise the down payment of 30 percent of the property value. The young pastor remembered a millionaire in Memphis who was interested in his ministry. He flew to Tennessee and had lunch with his friend, stating, "Everyone asks you for money; I only want you to *loan* me $15,000." He got his loan. The dream of the property had become a reality.

The total cost for the first anniversary day was $3,300, including rental of equipment, honoraria for speakers, and Colonel Sanders Kentucky Fried Chicken. Everyone had dinner on the grounds! No detail was overlooked, even to the rental of four portable toilets.

The church had been averaging $2,000 a week in offerings. That morning, over $4,000 was collected; the ushers used aluminum pie plates. The string section of the symphony played the offertory, to which the crowd gave silent nods of approval, just as they later enthusiastically applauded the rhythmic singing of The Inspirationals, a Southern quartet.

The spirit was electrifying and the congregational singing was enthusiastic. The crowd broke into spontaneous applause when teenagers from Dr. Purtle's former church lifted a huge banner for all to see: "First Baptist Church, Spring Hill, Louisiana; All Those Not Here, Wish They Were." Over 60 out-of-town visitors from those churches formerly pastored by Dr. Purtle showed up to join in the celebration.

Purtle realized that he could become preoccupied with getting new folks there and miss the purpose of the day. He spent all Friday alone, telling only his secretary where he could be located in case of emergency. He prepared his message and heart, asking God for spiritual power upon the day. He stated, "It would have been a mistake to have a great crowd and forget why we worked to get them here."

An old-fashioned gospel invitation followed the message. Seventeen adults responded to the invitation, several kneeling in the sawdust to receive Christ. The children met at the Aldridge Elementary School where 35 made decisions for Jesus Christ.

Purtle came to Richardson by faith, living without a salary for the first year. He had been pastoring in the Baptist Missionary Association but wanted to found an independent church; no organization backed the church. He immediately phoned his former Associate Pastor in Louisiana, Rev. Hughes, inviting him to come and help establish the church, explaining, "There is no salary, but I'll give you half of all God gives me." The inseparable friends formed a perfect team: Purtle, the man of vision; Hughes, the man of details. One member quipped, "When Purtle gets a headache, Hughes takes an aspirin."

The attendance of 1,103 is not the largest crowd for a first anniversary. Mid-way Baptist Church, Phoenix, Arizona, had 1,457 in 1969, but most were kids on buses. Canyon Creek had only two buses with less than 70 riders. Their goal was to get 200 new families.

PLANS FOR THE BIG DAY

Purtle began planning for the "Super Sunday" the day he founded the church. There was never a doubt in his mind that the church would grow. "I knew that if God would bless hard work, I could build a great church." Because of his success in other churches, Purtle worked with confidence and built with assurance. Many young pastors who begin a church lack assurance because they have never had a successful pastorate. Their announcements lack the ring of assurance that builds confidence in the followers. Purtle never doubted his ability to build a great church.

Three months before anniversary Sunday, he took his staff on an all-day retreat. There, he outlined everything to be done to get ready for anniversary Sunday. Some look at a high attendance day and wonder how a large crowd can be attracted. A large crowd is never attracted by prayer only or by the setting of goals. Hard work is the secret to growth. Purtle outlined the following program of hard work to attract 1,000 on anniversary Sunday.

1. *Build congregational expectation.* Purtle had "I Love 1,000" labels printed and distributed to the congregation. He instructed his people to stick the 2″ x 3″ labels on their mirrors

and books and post them around the room to remind them of their goal. These were distributed six months before the date, to stretch the expectation of the congregation.

2. *Everyone tell someone every day.* Purtle got the people to commit themselves to tell one person every day about the anniversary Sunday. This was not to invite people, but to create the excitement and get the city talking about the infant congregation.

3. *The 24-hour prayer chain.* A prayer clock was printed and each person was asked to sign up for 24 hours of continuous prayer the day before the anniversary Sunday.

4. *The telephone.* Pages of the Richardson telephone book were distributed, along with a printed solicitation. Every person in the city was phoned and invited to Sunday School.

5. *The church newspaper.* The church's newspaper *The Baptist Voice* was sent to every resident of Canyon Creek and many other residents throughout Richardson, telling them about anniversary Sunday.

6. *Bring a family.* Purtle asked the people to do more than bring visitors. Every teenager and adult was asked to be responsible to bring at least one family to the anniversary service.

7. *Establishment of goals.* Purtle set a goal of 200 visiting families on anniversary day, out of which he expected a minimum of ten to 20 families to join the church. (Only one family joined the church on that day, but another ten stopped him during dinner on the grounds to say, "This is the first time we've been here, but this is the kind of church we've been looking for." The church now has four families from that day.

A goal of 100 out-of-town visitors was set, along with 100 on the buses. He felt 200 visiting families would bring in 800 people, along with his 400 regulars. After he set the goals, he explained to his people "I know beyond the shadow of a doubt that we will reach 1,000." Unknown to his people, he was working for 1,200; 1,207 attended the morning service. His confidence bred enthusiasm, which in turn instilled confidence in workers.

8. *Mailing.* A typed letter was sent to every visitor who had been in the services of Canyon Creek Baptist Church, inviting them to return on anniversary Sunday.

9. *Commitment.* Three weeks before anniversary day, mimeographed cards were passed out and every person was asked to

commit himself to the number of families he would bring. The people committed themselves to bring 201 families, which matched the goal of 200 Purtle had set at the staff retreat.

10. *The under-shepherd ministry.* Purtle says the most effective technique to reach the multitude was the plan for "under-shepherds." These were the leaders of the church who followed up the goals and commitments made by members. Each under-shepherd was responsible for ten units. A unit is a family, whether the family consists of one or many. For three months, Purtle had been motivating each member to reach families. Now, the under-shepherds contacted every person who had made a commitment to motivate them to work to accomplish their goal. The pastor noted, "Someone besides me was motivating everyone to reach the goal."

11. *Assign individuals to responsibilities.* Purtle is not against committees but realizes that individuals accomplish more than a committee. He assigned jobs to people for parking cars, ushering, serving as hostesses, providing meal service, working in children's church and the nurseries. Each person was to recruit helpers for his task.

The entire morning service was recorded, and made into a long-play record album. A local company had a large trailer-van next to the tent, recording the service in stereo. Purtle sold many albums at the end of the service, helping to defray the cost of the day.

Getting members of the Dallas Symphony Orchestra involved persistence on the part of the pastor. Purtle talked to the president of the Musicians' Union, discovering that there was a foundation in the Dallas area that underwrote charity performances. He wrote a letter appealing for financial assistance, to get the musicians for the day. The reduced cost was approved by the union president, and financial help came from the foundation. The use of the orchestra cost the church only $330.

The new building, a large gymnasium-auditorium that will seat 500, is made of pre-stressed concrete. The platform where the pulpit is located will roll under the south stands. The permanent baptistry is built on the second-floor level overlooking the entire auditorium. One thousand can be seated in the gym. A two-story Christian education building is also being constructed to accommodate 600 in Sunday School. Eventually the church is planning a 2,500-seat auditorium.

Dr. Purtle had been pastor of Webb's Chapel Baptist Church, approximately 20 miles away. He had built the church from an attendance of 250 to a high attendance of 976. At the old church, he had expanded the bus ministry to 13 buses, with a high of 650 riders. Dr. Purtle left because he wanted to reach lost children on the buses, build a larger educational building and preach the gospel over radio and television. His vision was too great for some members of the church, and he recognized that if the people are not in harmony with the pastor they won't follow his leadership. He started Canyon Creek Baptist Church, testifying, "I have wanted to build an independent Baptist church all my life."

Purtle has a vision of building a great church on preaching and teaching the old-fashioned religion, yet making the facilities and organization as modern as possible. He has set a goal of having 2,000 on his second anniversary, with 5,000 by the fifth birthday of the church. "I don't know what we will do with the people," he confesses.

"If God will bless hard work, our goal will become a reality," stated Purtle. "The people have a vision and are ready to work."

Canyon Creek Baptist Church

CHAPTER SIX

A CHURCH IN THE LENGTH AND SHADOW OF ITS LEADER

TRI-CITY BAPTIST CHURCH
Tempe, Arizona
JIM SINGLETON, *Pastor*

The Tri-City Baptist Church, Tempe, Arizona, has emerged out of the burden and vision of its pastor and founder, Rev. James Singleton. Since it is difficult to understand a church apart from its leader, an examination of the influences that molded James Singleton will contribute to understanding of the church.

Jim Singleton came to know Christ through the instrumentality of a Plymouth Brethren Gospel Hall. He gained a zeal for evangelism as he read the exploits of John Wesley and the early circuit riders of the Methodist church, the place where he spent his boyhood and young manhood. Singleton gravitated to the Southern Baptist Convention, where he learned to build stability into a local church through the Sunday School. Finally, through the influence of the Baptist Bible Fellowship, he realized a church must be independent, pastor-led and doctrinally sound. Singleton has tried to incorporate all of his previously learned lessons into the church he founded in Arizona. Under the leadership of God, he has made the Tri-City Baptist Church into a youthful giant.

After four short years, Tri-City Baptist Church owns seven acres of ground at the corner of two main arteries, receives $2,200 a week in offerings, averages 542 in Sunday School, has built four buildings, has 190 students in a full-time Christian grade school, supports 25 staff members, and has reached a record at-

56

tendance of 741. Growth has come through a minimum amount of busing and a maximum use of laymen; a minimum amount of traditional church procedures and a maximum amount of New Testament principles.

James Singleton was born in Key West, Florida, 1927, and as a child attended a Methodist church where his grandfather taught Sunday School. He believed such doctrines as "immersion and the security of the believer." Young Jimmy went to the Methodist church on Sunday morning and again Sunday evening, but in the afternoon attended Sunday School in a Plymouth Brethren Gospel Hall. At age 12, he received the Lord during one of their special meetings. A layman preached on John 3:16 and, although there was no public invitation, Singleton received the Lord as he sat in the pew, testifying, "For the first time I understood the simple plan of salvation and believed in the Lord." As a teenager he grew through Bible study and went with Brethren youth passing out gospel tracts.

With plans to be a meteorologist, Singleton studied at Florida Southern College and finally ended up working for the Weather Bureau in Washington, D.C. Attending a Methodist church, he felt a growing conviction to be a preacher. After his speech at a youth meeting one night, an elderly lady told him, "You'd make a good minister." Inwardly he laughed but couldn't shake off her challenge.

He joined the Navy in 1945 as a weather forecaster. Even before shipping overseas, he had decided to go to a Christian college to study for the ministry. He mailed letters to Bob Jones University and Asbury College. He told God, "I'll go to the college that answers first." Within days the answer came from Bob Jones. After his discharge the following August, he went to Bob Jones University and finished within three years by taking a heavy load and attending summer school.

In the summer during college years, Singleton preached revival meetings anywhere he could get an invitation. After graduation, he began attending Bob Jones Divinity School while waiting for his wife, Mary, to finish college. That spring, all of his revival meetings were cancelled but one; at the same time a Methodist District Superintendent asked the young preacher to take a circuit of six churches in Fries, Virginia. "I felt the Lord was guiding me so I accepted the call, preaching in three churches one week and the

Pastor James Singleton

Tri-City Baptist Church

other three the following week." His $1,650-a-year salary couldn't support his family, so he accepted revival meetings to supplement his income.

Singleton had received baptistic convictions at Bob Jones and never sprinkled anyone at Fries, but always immersed converts after salvation. Of Baptists, he knew only the Southern Baptist Convention; hence, he drifted under their influence. He left the Methodist church to enter evangelism full time, knowing he couldn't go from a Methodist church to a Baptist church.

Next, Singleton received the B.D. and Th.M. degrees from Southeastern Baptist Theological Seminary in Wake Forest, North Carolina. For the next 14 years he served Southern Baptist churches in Atlanta, Georgia; Chattanooga, Signal Mountain, and Shelbyville, Tennessee.

"I became wrapped up in state-level Convention work, hoping to make the Southern Baptist Convention more conservative," testified Singleton. He served as Secretary of the Executive Board of Tennessee and Chairman of the Committee on Committees in addition to being a trustee for an educational institution. Working behind the scenes, Singleton attempted to get conservative pastors into places of leadership. However, during this time, growing liberalism disenchanted him.

When Singleton was ordained by a Southern Baptist church in 1953, an old pastor asked, "Young man, will you always be loyal to the Convention?" (The ordaining council knew of his Bob Jones background.) With prayer for wisdom, the young preacher replied, "Let me answer this way: As long as my Convention and my Lord walk hand in hand, I'll follow my Convention; but if the time ever comes that I feel they part company, you don't have to question twice which one I'll follow." Singleton didn't know how prophetic that statement was. Fifteen years later, disenchanted with the Southern Baptist Convention, he chose to follow his Lord.

Singleton wrote letters to the Southern Baptist papers, warning of a departure from the Word of God. His stand pegged him as a conservative. He looks back and testifies, "It would have been difficult for me to extricate myself from the Southern Baptist Convention in Tennessee. Now, I understand why God led me to Ohio."

Singleton had preached a revival in Ohio, and the state evangelist submitted his name as a candidate to several pastorless churches.

One Saturday, as he was in the family room praying, he received a long distance call from a pulpit committee in Ohio, asking if they could come and hear him preach. "Come ahead," Singleton told them, but also warned he was not interested in moving. The pulpit committee did come and invited Singleton to candidate in Ohio. While driving on the highway, he felt a strong sense of God's guidance and confided to his wife, "I believe this is where the Lord wants me." In subsequent conversation with her, he remarked that he would not get involved in state-level Southern Baptist work. Even then, there was a growing feeling he couldn't stay in the Convention.

One day Singleton visited Dr. John R. Rice to express his disturbed feelings about the Southern Baptist Convention, implying he would like to pastor an independent Baptist church.

"Brother Singleton," the wise editor of *The Sword of the Lord* commented, "when you leave the Convention, some of us will have confidence in you to help you get a church."

At the Lakeview Baptist Church, Vermilion, Ohio, Singleton tried to designate finances away from liberal Southern Baptist institutions; also, he tried to stop using Southern Baptist Sunday School material. In a compromise with his church, he wrote the Sunday School lessons for three months, then alternated and used Southern Baptist material for three months. Many in the congregation were not sympathetic with his independent tendencies, and there was a business meeting where some threatened to vote him out, although the impending confrontation never came about.

Singleton fellowshipped with Dallas Billington and Harold Henninger. Roy Thompson of Cleveland Baptist Temple took him to a Fellowship meeting at Springfield, Missouri. "God did not open up an independent church, but now I look back and see his plan," he explains. When Thompson suggested that Singleton start a church, he answered, "I am too old—past 40. I couldn't go through all the details."

Singleton took the First Baptist Church of Albion, Michigan (Conservative Baptist Association) for one year, but that restless conviction gnawed at him. "Should I really found a church?"

John Tucker, Youth Pastor of the Albion Church, was called to the Tucson Baptist Temple, Arizona, from which Pastor Louis Johnson phoned Singleton for a recommendation. As they chatted over the phone, Johnson casually invited, "Come to Arizona and visit us; the fields are white unto harvest. Start a church here."

Over the phone, Singleton raised several objections: "My church here has just bought ten acres of ground, hired an architect, and we're ready to build . . . I can't come." That was Wednesday morning. The following Monday morning Singleton got on an airplane for Arizona, testifying, "Until you have had God lead you, you can't explain the feeling of following him, yet the Lord led me to Arizona through that phone call from Louis Johnson." Even though Louis Johnson invited Singleton to Tucson, he got off the plane at Phoenix, looking up the only Baptist Bible Fellowship pastor he knew, Charles Vaden of the Alice Avenue Baptist Church. Since Vaden was out of town, Singleton made an appointment to see him the following morning.

Forty miles from Phoenix, in Tempe, was the Vaughn Adams family, who had been saved at Alice Avenue but found the distance too far to commute to Sunday services. They had been praying for someone to start a church in Tempe. Adams spent Wednesday with Singleton, showing him around the area. The burden to start a church in Tempe was growing. Singleton drove 100 miles to Tucson and talked with Louis Johnson, who agreed to help financially support the young church. Thursday evening, back in Tempe, Singleton met with three families, telling them, "I'll phone you on Monday." On the plane en route home, Singleton rationalized, "It would be easier for them to say no over the phone than to my face. If they say yes, I'll take it as a call from God." When he phoned the next Monday, they said, "If the Lord is leading you, we want you to come."

Singleton arrived in Tempe in August, 1969. There were 20 for the first service at the Adams' home—just three families, including the preacher's family. Three weeks later, they moved into Meyer Elementary School which became their church home for 24 months. Even though they looked at some old church buildings, Singleton didn't want the image of decay and stagnation. The new school building had refrigerated air and clean facilities. The School Board allowed the church to use the cafetorium, one large room. Singleton placed a Sunday School class in each corner. Since they could use the wide hallways, the people bought large screens, dividing the area for several classrooms and nurseries. Each week, they had to transport cribs, tables, screens and educational material.

From the very beginning, Singleton realized that Sunday School would be the agency to build a church, "reaching . . . teaching . . . winning . . . training." He met weekly with all the teachers, giving them instruction in both content and methodology. He personally recruited all teachers, stressing qualifications: salvation, church membership, tithing, attendance, pupil visitation, and separation from the world. Today he cautions young preachers, "It is a mistake to relax standards in the early days of a church because of pressure to get a church started, with a view to strengthening the teaching staff in the future." Then he notes, "I will sacrifice fast growth for stability and wait for God to send workers. We don't want to plant seeds that will damage the church in the future."

Some young preachers spend all their time evangelizing the lost, knocking on doors. Singleton says *balance* is the key to building a new church. He spent as much time visiting those outside his church as he did strengthening his members. The seasoned pastor didn't make the traditional pastoral calls, but visited in homes to teach his flock how the Tri-City Baptist Church was different. From the pulpit he cautioned prospective members not to be too quick to join his church (although the only requirements for membership were salvation and baptism). Singleton confessed, "I didn't want to appeal to disgruntled members from other churches and get myself bogged down with other pastor's problems."

When he visited prospective members he stated, "Since you have visited our church, I want to visit your home and welcome you to our fellowship. If the Lord wants you to join our church, we want you. If the Lord does not want you, we do not want you, and you would not be happy here." He suggested that new members not join if they found major policies they didn't like. "Ask all of your questions before you join," he stated. "Our way is not the only way, but this is the way our church is set up. We believe our church is biblical." Singleton explained that they did not have traditional deacon control; they did not have a committee structure; they were built around evangelism rather than worship, and members would be expected to live the Word of God. Today Singleton can testify, "As a result of our teaching in the home, we don't have a large turnover of membership nor do we have a large membership who never attend."

The new church needed property, and Singleton spent many hours looking for the correct location. It had to be: (1) easily accessible; (2) centrally located to the three cities (Tempe, Mesa, and Chandler—that's why it's called Tri-City); (3) not chosen because the ground was inexpensive or in an undesirable location; (4) at least ten acres; and (5) near a residential area where people were living, not out in the desert. Singleton prayed over a map and looked at every available property. He announced that the property had to be within one mile of Price and Southern Road. A member phoned to suggest the property on Price and Southern.

"That property is only one acre," Singleton told his parishioner.

"No, there's 6.9 acres behind that."

A contractor who had planned to build 14 houses there had recently died. The executor of the estate wanted $78,000.

The infant congregation had only accumulated $8,000 in the building fund and needed $20,000 for the down payment, to be paid within three months. The church had met for 13 months in the school building and were not sure they could raise $20,000 cash. Aware that they could lose their escrow, the people voted to pay $4,000 down and began trying to raise $20,000. A few days before closing, Singleton told the treasurer, "Pay all of our bills. Let's don't fool ourselves into thinking we've got money when we've left payables around the city." When the cash was counted, they had $17,300. Two men had told Singleton they had money to loan for a down payment; one loaned $1,000 and the other converted some bonds, raising $1,700—exactly $20,000.

"That $20,000 was the greatest miracle in the life of the church," Singleton testifies today.

The following spring they began selling a $100,000 bond issue. One April morning while shaving, Singleton had a burden on his heart. He told his wife, "The Lord wants us to start an academy . . . this fall." When he told the people, they agreed, but *this fall* stretched their faith. Yet, they voted by faith to proceed, assured the new academy was the will of God. That summer was hectic. They had to sell the bonds, construct the building, determine the curriculum, hire the teachers, and recruit the students. The teachers came from within the congregation, men and women who were teaching in the public school system. One teacher was criticized by a friend: "How can you open school in September? That building is only half done and this is July." With deep confidence and a pioneering spirit, she replied, "If the pastor says it will be finished, it will be finished."

Instead of the proposed two grades, the school expanded immediately to eight grades. Some people called Singleton "crazy." But God provided the teachers and pupils, and the contractor finished the five-room building before school opened. Two grades were assigned to each room and the four-teacher, eight-grade school got off the ground with 65 students.All teachers were state college graduates with deep convictions in Christian education.

From the beginning, the Tri-City Christian Academy has recruited many strong families for the church. Singleton has taken the stance: "If the academy hurts the local church, we will cut it off. Our primary concern is reaching our community through the church."

Sunday School was averaging under 200 when the congregation moved from the spacious cafetorium into their own building, a small four-classroom facility. Singleton stood in the hall and preached to people in two separate classrooms that first Sunday. The following week he divided the congregation into two services, at 9 A.M. and 11 A.M. Both services were quickly filled. Closed circuit television was needed because both services used two rooms. Today, Singleton disagrees with the Southern Baptist principle that demands space for Sunday School growth. "If people have the desire to expand, they can grow without space."

As soon as the church occupied the first building, they began constructing the second unit. The contractor divided the second building into five stages of completion. Singleton would not allow him to begin a stage until money was available through the sale of bonds. One Friday, Singleton phoned the contractor not to return the following Monday morning because there was no more money. The following day, two men from the church sold $5,000 worth of bonds to one customer, the largest single amount they had ever sold. Immediately, Singleton phoned the contractor to report for work the following Monday. They occupied that auditorium in April 1972, with $7,500 needed to complete payment. Enough bonds were sold on Dedication Day to pay off the builders. "We have literally built this church one step at a time," beams the pastor.

Immediately, Singleton wanted to build a third building, but no one would loan him money. He had met a bank manager at the Arizona Breakfast Club, who kept saying, "I'd like to come visit your church." The day the bank manager finally did visit, Singleton confidently announced to the people, "I think we will get a loan from a life insurance company and begin a third building." On the way out, the bank manager commented, "If you don't get your loan, come see me." When the life insurance company turned down Tri-City Baptist, Singleton told the manager he needed $100,000 to pay off the land and build a third building. The Western Savings Bank loaned the money and held the deed on the property. Eventually, the bank loaned them an extra $70,000 for cost override.

No sooner had they completed the third building than the congregation began the fourth auditorium to seat 650 people (116 x 40 ft.) at a cost of $45,000, or under $10.00 per square foot. Dedicated in September, 1973, the western-type building with rough brown exterior and a simple interior will seat 650 people in folding chairs, also providing the church with its first permanent baptistry.

Singleton meets with his teachers every Sunday evening at 6 P.M., forming the nucleus of growth. First, the pastor checks the attendance of his workers and those who are not there are followed up during the week. Singleton writes the Sunday School lesson for junior age and older, handing out a lesson plan to all teachers. He summarizes the lessons for the teachers, then promotes the Sunday School, motivating his teachers to excitement about the greatest task in life. During the last 20 minutes of the workers' meeting, the departmental superintendents meet with their teachers, discussing methodology and techniques for teaching.

Recently a visitor left the morning service, commenting, "I knew this was a special promotion day, but I didn't hear much about it in the morning service." Singleton's Southern Baptist background causes him to keep dignity in the church services. Promotion is restricted to the Sunday School; the morning service is reserved for preaching.

In the fall of 1973, four special days were planned, setting goals of 603, 653, 703, and then 1,003. These high goals came on the

Revival Congregation at Tri-City Baptist Church

first day of September, October, November and December. The first three goals were attained, but on the fourth target date for 1,003, only 723 attended Sunday School. Asked how he interprets failure to his people, Singleton stated,"We made three out of four goals. Whereas many churches set only one goal, we set four; this was much more difficult. We'll get 1,000 next spring." His people said, "*Amen*!!"

When faced with the question, "How do you build confidence in your leadership?" Singleton replied he tries to be certain that everything he does is God's will. "If God puts in the order, He will pay the bills." Singleton stresses *balance* in leading a church. He noted that the Sunday School could have grown faster through buses, but he wanted to build a solid financial basis under the church, train workers, supply space for adequate Bible teaching, and then add buses as the church can absorb the children.

Singleton's pulpit ministry is different from the average independent Baptist preacher. According to his people, he seldom, if ever, preaches just an evangelistic message. But in every sermon, there is enough salvation that the unsaved can receive the Lord. There is an invitation following every Sunday service.

Singleton indicated that a minister preaches differently in a new church than in an old congregation, indicating, "In an old congregation he can *get by* on theatrics, dramatics, or pulpiteering." He noted that a new congregation is built on meeting the needs of his people. Instead of topical sermons, Singleton is known for his practical messages. A member noted, "He reaches into issues where people live. I can apply almost every sermon he has preached." Singleton tries to combine biblical content and revival fire in every sermon, giving both doctrine and evangelism.

When the problem of tongues came up in the community (not in the church), he preached a series of four Sunday evening sermons, "What the Bible Teaches About the Holy Spirit." His approach was, "I didn't want to just blast tongues but to lay a biblical foundation for our stand against it." On another occasion, he preached six Sunday evening messages on the topic, "They Are After Your Child," indicating that new education, drugs, sensitivity training, sex education, radical movements and rock music are all after our children.

The second meeting that has built the church is the midweek

Tuesday meeting. It is not called "prayer meeting," because they do much more than pray. They don't meet on Wednesday because, in the early days in Meyer School, the midweek meeting was held in a rented business club available only on Tuesday. The people have grown accustomed to arranging their weeks around Tuesday, so the congregation continues to meet on that day.

For the first 15 minutes the midweek meeting centers around testimonies which Singleton says are more than "reviewing one's salvation." The people share burdens, give answers to prayer, tell lessons they have learned, or ask for prayer support concerning their problems. Three times each year a layman, Bob Fetters, teaches a series on soul-winning to new members. The others are in an advanced soul-winning class conducted by the pastor. Recently, he finished a series on Jehovah's Witnesses, entitling it "How to Witness to a Witness." Another series was "How to Help People with Problems," stating that after they had led people to the Lord, they must learn how to minister to their problems.

While the pastor is speaking, a clipboard wtih the words "Yes/No" is passed around the auditorium. Those who have a partner for visitation signify *yes;* those without a helper are matched up for soul-winning. College students are paired up with their age group; high school students visit with their age group. Singleton calls his midweek service a "work night." The people spend approximately 15 minutes in prayer and, from 8:00 until 9:30 P.M., the entire church goes soul-winning. During a recent month, Tuesday visitation attendance averaged from 122 to 161. The pastor observed, "Our midweek service has kept our spirits growing and our numbers expanding." When some claim that visitation is short, Singleton answers, "We might have more time on another night but fewer people would visit."

Singleton has made extensive use of local newspapers to advertise the church. The church ads do more than advertise the time and place of meetings. Paid-for space is used to share news, growth, philosophy, and new items in the church. Once the ad read: "When driving by—watch our new building go up." On another occasion: "Sorry we couldn't seat everyone last Sunday evening. Our new auditorium is on the way." Again, "Our new singles class is busting at the seams." During a session on the Christian home, he advertised his topic and philosophy of the Christian family.

Singleton tells young preachers, "Next to my Bible, I study my financial statement most." He tries to make his people cost-conscious because, to him, *money is ministry:* "The way we handle our money is the way we handle our ministry." He lists some very simple rules for the young preacher starting out: (1) Don't spend more money than you take in. (2) Income should increase in proportion to membership. (3) Always know how much money you have in all accounts. (4) Keep good credit in the community; pay all your bills or arrange for extension.

CHAPTER SEVEN

"THE VALLEY'S MOST EXCITING CHURCH"

BEREAN BAPTIST CHURCH
Salem, Virginia
RUDY HOLLAND, *Pastor*

When I arrived the first time in Roanoke, Virginia on February, 1971, Jerry Falwell whisked me from the airplane over to U. S. 460, pointing me to the east of the four-lane highway to a 10.5 acre field. "You're going to see a great church there." Falwell explained that Rudy Holland, a young man from Thomas Road was building a new church. At that time, the only thing on the property was a red barn, a chicken coop, a small utility house and a 100-year old home where Holland lived. Today, a huge black and orange sign "Berean Baptist Church," illuminates the darkness, announcing to passers-by: "The Valley's Most Exciting Church." It also boasts Roanoke's largest Sunday School.

Today, Berean Baptist Church averages over 650 in Sunday school, has 700 members and receives a weekly offering of $3,200. The church had a peak attendance of 1,069 in May, 1973 and has aggressively notified the city of its plans and services. In the four years of existence, the church has gone through four building programs. Holland pointed to the red mud around the latest excavation. "We'll always have that." The total worth of assets is $450,000 on which $350,000 is owed.

The unbelievable growth of the church is a story of a young man with an indomitable will. He invariably has a strand of hair on his forehead and has been described as a "bulldog for God," one who would drag people kicking, into the Kingdom.

Rudy Holland was born in Kenly, North Carolina. His dad, a

70

tenant farmer, worked in the shipyard at Newport News during the war. When Rudy was 13, his father moved to Lynchburg, Virginia where the family attended Thomas Road Baptist Church. Young Holland confesses, "I never got saved as a young boy, but planned to." At age 16 he got a job at Archie's Lobster House and in a short time, became kitchen manager and a trusted employee for the elderly Archie Parrish. Holland often asked to work on Sunday so he wouldn't have to go to church.

As he looks back on his Christian home, he indicates, "I never knew what it meant not to attend church or to sit down to a meal and not pray." Two years later, his father built a home three doors from Jerry Falwell, and the daily influence of the senior pastor made an indelible impression on Rudy Holland.

The week before his salvation, Rudy went to a dance in Bedford, 25 miles from Lynchburg. He had been drinking heavily and, with bottled courage, decided to crash the party, even though he had been warned to stay away. Several Bedford boys decided to teach Rudy and his buddy a lesson. They brought out knives and chains, but the Bedford police arrived to prevent an ugly scene.

The haunting thought of death lingered in Rudy's mind and with pressure from his parents, he attended a Lester Roloff revival at Thomas Road Baptist Church in April, 1965. As the congregation sang the invitation, his muscles tensed and he fiercely gripped the back of the pew in front of him.

"I'll go with you Son," said his mother. Rudy stepped out at once and was met at the altar by a white-haired gentleman, Mr. Mayberry (still active in Thomas Road), who led him to Christ.

The youth director of the church talked Holland into going to Tennessee Temple Schools. His roommate, Dan Manley, had prayed for Rudy's salvation two years before he was saved. Dan had been dating Rudy's sister. At first, Rudy was miserable at college; God was dealing with his heart. He talked to a number of professors about going into full-time Christian service. One night, Rudy asked his roommate what he should do. Dan said, "Your answer is in the Word of God."

Since First Timothy was written to a young preacher, Holland began reading there to find his answer. In high school, he had poor academics, had gotten involved in sin, and had been a foul-

Pastor Rudy Holland

mouthed teenager. Then he read, "And I thank Christ Jesus our Lord, who hath enabled me for that he counted me faithful, putting me into the ministry" (I Tim. 1:12). The word *putting* stood out in his mind; God would put him in the ministry. The next verse had equal weight; "Who was before a blasphemer, and a persecutor, and injurious; but I obtained mercy because I did it ignorantly in unbelief" (v. 13). Here, the words *blasphemer* and *ignorantly* also characterized his life. At the missions conference, Holland went forward to surrender for full-time Christian service. He doesn't remember who was preaching, but cannot forget Dr. Lee Roberson asking in front of that great auditorium, "Has God called you into the ministry?" His answer was "Yes." The fatherly Roberson continued, "Then you preach the Word and God will use you." Roberson looked out over the audience and said, "Thank God for this young man."

Immediately, Rudy Holland began driving 70 miles one way to teach Sunday School and lead singing in a small church. Next, he worked at the Skyline Bible Conference at Dayton, Tennessee, where he held a Saturday night youth conference. During that year, 70 teens made decisions for Christ. Holland confessed, "Not working in a local church bothered me. Even though I won 70 to the Lord, I didn't know where they were." So young Rudy went to work at Hinkle Baptist Church on Lookout Mountain where "Pastor Jimmy Lilly taught me to pray and to love people." There, Holland preached the funeral of a 15-year-old boy he had led to the Lord. Still in his Bible are the names of 23 young people who were saved at the graveside.

In his senior year of college, Holland wrestled to find the will of God about starting a church in Roanoke. Dan Manley and Holland came home the second week in February, 1970 and on their way to Lynchburg, passed Roanoke. Manley was driving and Holland looked out over Roanoke from Interstate 81 and saw "lights all over the place at 1:00 A.M."

"That's my mission field," declared Rudy. He began to cry. Dan Manley said, "Amen". In Lynchburg, Holland intended to ask Falwell's advice on where to go, but instead asked, "How can I get started in Roanoke?"

Falwell said, "Just move, and start knocking on doors."

He did just that.

After graduation, Rudy went to Roanoke looking for a place to start a church. He naturally went back to see his old friend at the Lobster House.

"Hello, Pop, do you remember me?" Rudy asked when he walked into the place. Rudy had been in college for five years and had not seen Pop.

"You're Holland," the old owner said to Rudy." I need a manager, and I'm too old to run this place." Archie asked Rudy to come and run the business.

"No! I'm in a new business—I want to start a church."

Archie remembered Holland as a rebellious lad with a foul mouth. He couldn't believe the change in Rudy.

"I want to rent one of your rooms to start a church," young Holland looked hopefully at the old man who was dying of cancer.

"I won't rent space to an old friend, but I'll let you meet free in one of my rooms." The next Sunday when Holland arrived, Archie had set up the large second-floor room for church. Young Holland remembers standing on the balcony overlooking the parking lot and praying, "Lord, will anyone come?" A little black Volkswagen came around the corner. Holland can point to the exact spot where it parked. Out scrambled the Frank Gordon family: father, mother, and two children. They formed the first Sunday's congregation with Holland's wife, mother, sister and husband and little girl—nine that first week.

The church met only one week at Archie's. The smell of cooking lobster coming up the stairs, plus the fact they couldn't get a piano up to the second floor, forced them to move.

That first evening the group moved to the auditorium of radio station WKBA. Two other ladies joined the infant congregation, Mrs. Kathleen Foster (now deceased) and Mrs. McKee. The small band of people met in the radio auditorium for six weeks, but finally had to move. The room would only hold 25 people.

For the first three months, Holland lived with his folks in Lynchburg, 50 miles away. He commuted to Roanoke for services and visitation. Jerry Falwell, who lived three houses away, stopped him in the middle of Grove Road one day and stuck a paper out of the window: "Visit this man. He will make you a great family." Larry Davis has been in the church since that day.

Holland remembers the days at WKBA auditorium. He preached week after week and no one was saved. There were three men in the church: John Heath, Larry Davis, and Frank Gordon. Each night he went visiting with a different man, but still no one was saved. The only result in the WKBA auditorium was a visiting teenager. After an evening service, Holland was chatting with some teens on the parking lot and began witnessing to her when she received the Lord.

The church was organized on August 28, 1970 with 17 charter members. Jerry Falwell came to Northside High School auditorium and held a two day revival. "That revival put our church on the map," Holland observed. Falwell was well known through television and the large Thomas Road Baptist Church. The meeting closed out on Saturday night. The following Sunday the church moved to a side room in the Salem Civic Center.

Attendance jumped from 25 to 40 when the congregation oc-

cupied the Civic Center. But the Sunday night meeting was unbearable at times. On hockey nights, the crowd forced the young
congregation to park a quarter of a mile away. During the rodeo
season, horses were led up and down the halls as Holland tried
to preach. During a rock concert, all types of hippies wandered
in and out of the service. Asked why they used the Civic Center
at all, "It was the only place we could find," reasoned the determined pastor. He explained that the city of Roanoke would not
cooperate in supplying a school building or other facilities. During
those days, the congregation made curtains to section off a Sunday
school room in each corner, making five classes. Curtains were
kept in the car trunks of some of the members.

Some came and stayed to help; others wouldn't consider the
group of people a church. "You're just a group of people meeting
in a Civic Center. When you get a building, we'll come," one observed.

Another problem was to convince the community that they
were not a mission of the Thomas Road Baptist Church. Holland
stated in a newspaper interview, "We are an independent, indigenous Baptist church. Even though Jerry Falwell participated in
my ordination, we have no organic link with Thomas Road Baptist
Church."

Others would not come because they felt Holland, only 23
years old at the time, was too young to be a pastor.

Holland had several realtors looking for property and had
viewed many large tracts of ground throughout the city. One
visitation day he noticed a weather-beaten board with "For Sale"
painted in red. He went around the corner and asked the farmer
how much. The answer was "$79,000." But the old gentleman said
he would reduce it to $75,000 for a church.

Holland prayed about the 11.5 acres and the more he prayed,
the greater peace he had. When he checked the city zoning, they
indicated a future road was planned through the middle of the
property, so they could not issue a building permit without the
approval of the Highway Department.

"No wonder I can't sell this property," the elderly farmer said
when he learned City Hall was holding up building permits.

Holland feels God providentially preserved the property for him
by allowing the city zoning department to give out the wrong infor-

Young People at Berean Baptist Church

mation. He was the only one who went to the Highway Department, where an official indicated they would not open the road until 1985.

"Hallelujah!" he said to the clerk. "We can use this for a church until then, and Jesus might even come back sooner." The Highway Department assured him if the church built a million dollar building on the property, the congregation would get their money back if it was condemned, plus 6 percent interest.

The following Sunday, Holland and the congregation went to the building site after the morning service. He stood on a rail fence and read from Joshua, "Let the feet of the priest step in the water." The small congregation knelt to claim the property for God. The neighbors who watched the strange procession never in their wildest imagination dreamed that within the next four years, four buildings would be erected there.

Jerry Falwell told Rudy Holland to offer $55,000 for the property, but if he had to, go as high as $65,000. There was a light rain falling when Holland drove up. The owner was sitting in a porch swing. When the old man said, "I must have $60,000," Holland swallowed his excitement and with a poker face, said, "I guess we'll have to go that high." In the deal, the church secured a built-in sewerage connection, with a twelve-foot sewerage drop so a basement could be built on the property.

The farmer agreed to finance the property at 6 percent on semi-annual payments. The young church paid $15,000 for one acre, secured an option on the rest, then sold $50,000 first mortgage bonds for a building. Within the next six months, they issued a second issue for $20,000 and a third for $50,000. Today, the entire 10.5 acres and buildings are under a first mortgage bond.

The congregation had averaged 178 in attendance at the Civic Center. The day they walked into the new building on their own property, 250 attended the dedication service. Attendance dropped to 190 for a few weeks, but things soon began to pop. Those who had only visited the Civic Center began attending regularly at the new property. Excitement spread over the congregation and tithing church families began joining. Giving doubled within a few months. At the end of the first year they were averaging 350 and, at the end of the second year, 610.

Contemplating the fantastic growth, Holland explains, "God

only does for a church what they expect. Most congregations don't expect much, so they don't have much. Most churches have a dime store religion because they have a dime store God. My God is rich."

Originally, the church built a 100' x 60' auditorium to seat 400 people. Next, they built a two-story educational wing, 48' x 30', then duplicated that building within six months. Today, they have an additional 60' x 60' two story educational wing.

Holland did not receive a salary for the first 15 weeks in Roanoke. Living by faith, he saw God answer many prayers. One night he prayed, "Lord, I need $25.00 for a phone hookup." The next day, there was a money order for $25.00 in the mailbox.

After 15 weeks he accumulated $450.00 in bills, and the situation was getting desperate. His wife, Doris, sat on the floor cleaning the storm door and broke down crying. She prayed, "Lord, we worked our way through college, paying all our bills. Why don't you answer our prayers?" She remembers praying, "Rudy's trying to start this church and he believes you will supply our needs."

The next morning his father handed him $125.00 which was his monthly tithe to help toward the bills. During the morning service, people began slipping money to Rudy Holland in five and ten dollar bills, amounting to $175.00. That evening, the deacons asked Rudy to leave the room while they talked with the congregation. Knowing the young preacher's needs, they agreed to immediately give him half of the general fund, which was $300. Also, the congregation agreed to pay him $75.00 a week, plus an extra love gift that month. After young Holland added it all together, he had enough to pay his $47.00 tithe, pay off all his bills and take his wife out to a restaurant. "That was the greatest miracle of my life," observed the young pastor. Within six months his salary was raised to $135.00 a week, and later, raised again. In its second year, the church added two full-time staff members.

The church believes in advertising, splashing its phrase, "The Valley's Most Exciting Church" on bumper stickers and numerous billboards throughout the valley. A number of people first attended the church because of one-minute commercials on local television or radio. Holland states, "We believe in using every available means to get people to come under the sound of the gospel. We stress a people-centered, not a program-centered church. We try to give people something to do when they get here, helping each other in all kinds of practical ways."

The church has the largest Sunday School bus ministry in the valley, bringing approximately 300 persons in 12 vehicles; 481 bus riders attended on its third anniversary.

The church is more than super-aggressive; it has been called "Super-growth" by the *Roanoke News*. It received $23,000 in the first year; $69,000 in the second year, and during the first five months of the third year, giving exceeded $65,000. The local newspaper stated, "Because of its rapid growth, it is difficult to write about a church like Berean Baptist without becoming lost in superlatives. And that makes the news column sound like paid advertisement."

Some of the other churches in the valley are jealous of the Berean Baptist Church. The *News* stated, "Members and ministers of other churches are jealous of the independent super-aggressiveness. They dismiss it as superficial at best; robbery at worst."

Someone asked Holland why he started a church instead of looking for a congregation that needed a pastor and already had a building. "It is easier to give birth than to raise the dead," he replied. "If I had taken a church of 100 I wouldn't be this large today. Demolition takes time; I would have had to tear down an old structure and re-educate the people."

Holland looks back and suggests that a young preacher should start the church the way he wants it to continue to be operated. The first Sunday, he organized into Sunday School classes. His wife taught the class for children and he taught the adults. He indicated they conducted their first services for nine people the same as if they had 500 with singing, announcements, prayer and preaching. Holland comments, "People do not like to change, so organize your services right and you won't have to change."

From the very beginning, Rudy Holland led the congregation in an aggressive program of soul winning. He indicates, "I started with enthusiasm and we still have it." That first Sunday he instilled in his people vision, telling them that within five years they would have 5,000 in Sunday School—the same rate of growth as Thomas Road.

When the church built its first building, Holland told them, "That's just an educational building with a temporary auditorium," even though it would seat 400. Frank Gordon, the first member of the church was going to a funeral with another preacher in town. As the funeral cars passed Berean Baptist Church, the clergyman asked, "Why are you building such a large building for such a small congregation?" Gordon responded with typical Berean Baptist faith, "Oh, that's only the educational building. We'll build a larger auditorium later."

Holland has tried to instill an attitude of growth in his people. Anything other than expansion would be a traumatic experience to the infant congregation. The attitude of the people suggests just that.

CHAPTER EIGHT

I WAS NEVER AFRAID OF FAILURE

FOX RIVER VALLEY BAPTIST CHURCH
Aurora, Illinois
GEORGE ZARRIS, *Pastor*

George Zarris is the youngest pastor in this book, yet has started a church in an area of larger population concentration than the other churches mentioned in this book. The Fox River Valley Baptist Church has built an attendance that averages over 575, yet doesn't have a permanent building. Mass media was not used to publicize opening day. Zarris and his wife just went door to door winning souls. His principles are different because he is not like the other nine men in this book. Yet, there is a similarity of pattern with the others because all men agree on basic fundamental doctrine.

George Zarris was born in Chicago, December 31, 1949. He didn't attend church as a boy although his father attended the Greek Orthodox Church. When in elementary school, the family moved to Dolton, Illinois, where a relative invited him to Lorimer Baptist Church. George walked four blocks each week to Sunday School. When he was 11 years of age, he was under conviction for a number of weeks. Since no one went forward in that church, he didn't. During a devotional at Christian Service Brigade, George and his brother, Gary, raised their hands for salvation. The leader told them, "If you really want to get saved, I'll talk to you afterwards." The boys said, Yes. Later, in the cafeteria, George Zarris received the Lord.

When he was 15 years old, a relative invited him to the First Baptist Church of Hammond, Indiana. At first, young George

Pastor George Zarris

didn't like Dr. Hyles, accusing him of "ranting and raving." Zarris remembers the sermons being long and loud. Even so, young George was under conviction because he was not living for Christ. Baptism was also an issue because he had not been immersed. At Lorimer, they had to be interviewed by the deacons before baptism. Zarris attended at least three more times, then went forward for rededication and baptism. Immediately, he quit going with a Catholic girl which he considered a big step of faith in his life. He immediately began soul-winning with the other young people in the church.

George was planning to attend a northern Christian college when he went in for his senior interview with Dr. Jack Hyles who told him, "Tennessee Temple Schools is the greatest preacher training school in the world." Zarris went there as a freshman in 1967, getting his B.A. degree in 1971 and M.R.E. degree in 1972, finishing six years of school in five years.

He looks back and remembers no great call into the ministry, "No lightening out of heaven." Young George testified, "I was a soul-winner, which is the greatest calling in life, and I wanted to do it full time. I just knew I was to be a preacher."

Between his freshman and sophomore year, George was driving down the Stevenson Expressway on the south side of Chicago when his father remarked, "It will be great when you get out of school and get a church in Chicago."

"No way . . ." young George told his father.

Approximately a month later, they were again driving down Stevenson Expressway when George remembered the words of his father. He looked out over the city and saw the steeples of dead churches and the number of Catholic churches. At that moment, he felt impressed to return to the Chicago area. That determination remained constant for the next four years.

While working in one of the chapels of Highland Park Baptist Church in Chattanooga, Zarris saw the problems of old Christians and the difficulty of inspiring old churches to win souls. He also saw the problem of changing the reputation of a church. He testifies, "I determined then to start my own church." During his last year of college, he knew he was going to start a church in Chicago and began making mental preparations to return to the windy city.

George invited Grant Rice over to his apartment for a meal. (Grant Rice was instrumental in helping three churches in this book.) Rice instructed young Zarris on how to prepare a church constitution, how to choose an area and how to go about founding a church. In March, 1972, Zarris returned to Hammond to the Pastors' Conference of First Baptist Church. One evening he drove to the Chicago area with Rice looking for an area to start a church. He was looking for (1) a high population area; (2) an area that didn't have a growing fundamental church; (3) an area where land was available for future expansion, and (4) a place where they could rent a building or auditorium. Steve Frankenberger flew George over the city of Aurora in his plane. They couldn't tell much from the air but, in that small plane with his wife, Barbara, George determined that Aurora was the area. Rice was not in the plane but had previously related the fact, "Fox River Valley will be the center of the population of the state of Illinois by 1980." The Sunday *Chicago Tribune* supported the decision with an article on the front page discussing a multi-million dollar shopping center in Aurora.

On the plane, the three determined the name of the church— "Fox River Valley Baptist Church." Zarris remembered the admonition of Rice to make the name mean something: *"Say* what you want to *do."* Zarris had a desire to reach the entire valley.

The next day they stopped at the first bank they saw (the Valley National Bank) and opened an account. When the cashier asked for signees, Steve was appointed treasurer.

During the last two months of school, George finished the constitution and ended his student pastorate at the Maranatha Baptist Church of Tracy City, Tennessee. Immediately, he began sending tithes to Aurora. Steve Frankenberger added his tithes and those of George's father. During the next six weeks, they accumulated $500 before the church's first meeting.

Zarris also sent out a letter asking for money from friends and relatives. He admitted this was a flop. They received two $10 offerings. Dr. Jack Hyles committed the First Baptist Church to $200 a month for six months. This money went into capitalization to purchase equipment and supplies.

Zarris's father said he would help out for one year at $25.00 a week, warning, "If this thing isn't self-supporting by then, don't expect another penny from me!" "My dad put me against the wall and backed me into a corner. As I look back, his challenge was a blessing. It made me work."

Zarris moved into Aurora June 6 and held two or three Tuesday night services. This Bible study met in his upstairs apartment with 11 to 17 people attending.

The church had its first service on July 9, 1972, with 32 people present and an offering of $230.00. The church was self-supporting from the beginning. George Zarris was paid $150.00 a week including his salary, car, housing and utilities. Two ladies walked the aisle that first Sunday. George and his wife had led the two to the Lord in their homes.

Zarris printed no special flyer as did other churches in this book. "We went door to door, trying to win people to Christ." They did not try to advertise nor "circularize" the community. A small mimeographed leaflet gave the basic statistics of the church, but it was not a special announcement of a new church organizing in the community. Zarris also indicates that there were no paid ads in the paper nor radio announcements. He gave a news release to the newspaper which included it as a news item. Two families phoned to ask what church they had split from. (One family joined as a result of the news release but has since moved to Arizona.)

Zarris asked the public school officials to rent him a school building. "We told them we were going to build a growing church and eventually their facilities wouldn't be big enough." The Greenman Elementary School was rented, and George and Barbara went door to door around the school, talking to people about Christ.

The First Baptist Church of Hammond, sent songbooks and and 100 chairs for the first service. Attendance grew in the first two months.

July 9	32
July 16	28
July 23	30
July 30	24
August 6	27
August 13	31
August 20	36
August 27	48

During the last week of August, George taught on separation, explaining Biblical standards. He indicated that the ladies who taught in Sunday School could not wear slacks or miniskirts; the men could not have long hair. Workers could not attend the movies. No one walked out on the young pastor; they just got hot and mad. Zarris indicates his congregation was young and carnal. That week he lost half of his congregation.

In counseling with Dr. Hyles, the wise preacher pointed out his mistakes. "Recruit your teachers individually. Don't embarrass them publicly and run them out of the church." Zarris confesses to his ignorance in handling the matter. He still has the same standards and says, "I'd split over the same issue, but I would do it differently." Hyles advised, "If the church was in a small town, he would have blown it, but Aurora can absorb the mistakes of a young man." Since that time, some have come back to the church.

For the first two years, there were no deacons in the church. Someone accused the church of being unscriptural. Zarris answered, "It would be a greater mistake to get unscriptural deacons than have the office go unfilled. Since he wanted pure leadership, he led the singing and taught the adults and youth for six months. He indicated no one was qualified. (We now have over 30 teachers and 11 bus captains who meet the qualifications.)

Zarris advises a young man to get the preparation work done before arriving on the field. This includes getting the constitution written and incorporation papers in order (no lawyer is needed to incorporate in Illinois). Zarris states, "Get your paperwork done so you can visit 60 hours a week on the field."

Zarris began full time immediately. Money for salary and expenses from other churches was not accepted; he didn't want his people to become "welfare Christians." (Money from First Baptist Church was used for capitalization.) Zarris explained, "I didn't want my people to live off the gifts of others." He immediately preached tithing and told the congregation it was their obligation to support the church. Zarris notes, "Most young preachers have to see where all of the money is coming from before they begin a church." He feels this is wrong. "The more a young church trusts God, the faster it will grow."

Within a year, the church took on partial financial support of four missionaries who were starting four new churches—two in Wisconsin, one in Illinois and one in Indiana. All four of these churches are now prospering. Three other churches are underway. Already, Fox River Valley Baptist Church has helped start seven churches. Grant Rice is one of four new missionaries he is helping start new churches.

"I was never scared in starting a church," testified Zarris. "I had First Baptist Church background and knew I could win souls." He testifies that anybody who grows up in Hammond has the inner assurance that he can build a church.

Zarris tells a young man that the most important ingredients in building a church are faith, works, and a helpmeet—"in that order." The wife had better be a soul-winner, or a man can't establish a church. At first, Barbara went with him. Now, she goes soul-winning with the ladies while George goes with the men.

The church was organized on September 10, 1972, in what Zarris calls "The Constitution Signing Service." Grant Rice preached and those who wanted to be charter members came forward to sign the constitution. They had to be saved and baptized before they could join. Only six signed. "We technically became a church that evening," testifies Zarris.

After the split, Zarris announced a goal of 100 in Sunday School. Even his wife thought 100 was too high. He noted, "The people didn't say the goal was too high, but their faces said it." Without buses, they began reaching out into the community and hit 57 the first week, 71 the next week, 105 the third week and only dropped under 100 in attendance once again, with a high of 173 on the last Sunday of the fall campaign. In that push they averaged 108.

During the campaign, Jack Nelson used his station wagon and brought 16 to Sunday School. Later, Jack Nelson and Pastor Zarris were visiting and came to the last house for the day. A white Plymouth station wagon pulled in right before they came to the house. A Spanish lady got out of the car. The Pastor and Jack asked the lady if her children could ride to church in their station wagon. She said they were her sister's children and not hers. She asked them if they wanted her station wagon.

"I thought she was upset," replied Pastor Zarris and talked to her sister about the children coming to Sunday School.

The woman who owned the car said, "I'm going to give you this - - - car or blow it up."

"You don't want to give me that car—you're just mad." The young preacher tried to talk calmly to her. She prevailed and they drove to her house, got the title, went to the bank and had it notarized. (The children came that Sunday in Jack's station wagon.)

"That white Plymouth got our bus ministry vitalized."

Later, they heard about a church bus for sale for $100. Zarris went downstate Illinois with Jack Nelson and towed it to Aurora, it was overhauled and immediately began bringing in riders.

To this day, the buses are painted emergency orange with a white stripe and black fenders. When asked about the colors, George Zarris replied, "Because others were stealing our riders," Now, no one gets on a church bus by mistake. Emergency orange also reminds people that they are "rescue vehicles for eternity."

One of the present problems of the young congregation is meeting in a school building that is too small. They still don't have

The Congregation of Fox River Valley Baptist Church

their own building. They rented a house as a rallying point and averaged 70 in their Tuesday evening Bible study. The office is on the first floor and services are held in the basement. The teens meet in the buses during the winter for their Sunday School class.

The church is buying 17 acres on Randall Road, the fastest north-south route in the county. They searched for property for six months when Mrs. Molen mentioned the property for sale on Randall and Oak Streets. A dirty old sign advertised the property. Born-again Lutheran people had been asking $9,000 an acre, but are selling it to the church for $100,000 or $6,000 an acre.

The church has seen 12 to 15 young preacher boys from the congregation called into the ministry. In the fall of 1974, they have approximately 12 going away to Christian schools (both boys and girls).

The church uses the master teacher plan because of limited facilities. There is one teacher for each department, with assistants responsible for teaching the verses, leading the singing, or looking after details. The weekly teachers' meeting is conducted both on Tuesday morning and evening because of shift work. Zarris teaches the lesson to his teachers. Some classes number up to 100, but there are few discipline problems because of the adult helpers.

Zarris noted, "Our people don't know defeat. We have always been successful." He pointed out that the young Christians have never learned bad habits. As an example, if someone leaves after Sunday School, they come and ask him for permission to leave. About half of the congregation have been won to Christ; the other half come from dead churches. Zarris relates, "The excitement of our church makes them feel this is the way Christians ought to act." George is an explicit preacher, and potential church members know what they are getting into before they join. "I tell potential members they will be trained to be soul-winners so they fit in when they become members."

"My goal was to average 1,000 at the end of three years—to win one person per day in my ministry at Fox River Valley." The young preacher looks at his goal and explains, "We are planning on averaging 900 to 1,000 this fall in the school. We will put all our boys' classes on buses." He also set a goal to be the largest Baptist church in the city. That goal has been reached. The only church larger is a Presbyterian church.

The church has met most of its attendance goals. In the spring of 1973, they set a goal to average 251 for the ten weeks; they averaged 274. In the spring of 1974, they set a goal to average 611 in Sunday School with a final attendance of 1,000. This was called, "March to Millennium." During the last week of the campaign, the ladies phoned everyone in the city; three mass mailings went to the city; the Tuesday Bible study went door to door visiting; Wednesday, more soul-winners went on the regular visitation services, and, on Thursday, Zarris set a goal of 100 persons to go visiting. The church took a full-page advertisement in the local paper. On May 19, 1974, they had an attendance of 1,105 in Sunday School and 1,155 in the morning service.

Zarris presently spends ten hours a week in soul-winning and visitation. When the church was young, he could spend 40 hours weekly, but now he must give more time to administration. He states, "The secret to growth is soul-winning; the secret to holding people together is standards."

"I am as hard as Dr. Hyles. Our people know what we require and why. They fill out a Christian leader qualification sheet indicating they will live by the standards, try to win souls, tithe, and attend teachers' meetings and all of the services." The young preacher counsels his people, "If you can't keep our standards, let me know. I don't want to fire anyone."

Some of the churches in the city have publicly criticized the Fox River Valley Baptist Church. Zarris rationalizes, "Every time they criticize us, they advertise our ministry. Their people come to see what we are all about." When a lady joined the church and requested her letter, the pastor attacked the Fox River Valley Baptist Church from his pulpit. Zarris thought to himself, "How foolish. Since he's not doing anything, he is telling dissatisfied Christians that we *are* doing something."

Zarris talks about the loneliness of starting a new church. "I felt lonely those first few weeks because I had no one in my church. As I told everyone I was starting a church, I suddenly realized I was somebody—I was a child of the King. I was doing something no one else was doing. I was starting a church." That self-image supported him in his loneliness.

Some advise a young preacher not to socialize with his people, but Zarris comments, "The only thing our church had for permanent headquarters was a small three-bedroom townhouse where we lived. Our people were at our home constantly for two years. The teens came there for choir practice, and all the visitation teams met in our living room. The bus workers came on Saturday morning, and the whole church gathered there on Tuesday evening." Zarris testifies of a bond that grew between him and his people because of using his house as headquarters.

Zarris comments that Jack Hyles preached a sermon that has motivated him to pray daily for power, wisdom and love. Then he noted, "I ask for these three things every day. I want God to give me wisdom beyond my years so I can be an effective pastor."

CHAPTER NINE

THE USE OF MONEY IN STARTING A CHURCH

FLORENCE BAPTIST TEMPLE
Florence, South Carolina
BILL MONROE, *Pastor*

The use of money in starting a church is more important than anything else except the use of people. But in the final analysis, a leader's attitude toward people will influence the way he handles finances. The Florence Baptist Temple has experienced phenomenal growth for many reasons. One of the church's strengths is Pastor Bill Monroe's attitude toward money.

The Florence Baptist Temple was begun in November 1969. Four years later, attendance averages over 900 in Sunday School with a high day of over 1,600 on June 2, 1974, and a weekly offering over $4,000. The Christian Day School enrolls 400 pupils up through grade eight. The modern, streamlined $700,000 facilities on US #301 contains an auditorium seating 1,200 with Sunday School space for over 1,000 students on ten acres of ground. All of this is an unthinkable attainment for a four-year-old church.

Bill Monroe had a deep feeling that God was calling him into the pastorate. He had read *The Ten Largest Sunday Schools* many times and concluded, "If Dallas Billington could work in a rubber factory and build the largest Sunday School in the world, why not me?" Monroe had sung in a gospel quartet, traveling over America, and knew these large churches. Being music director for Dr. Greg Dixon at Indianapolis Baptist Temple no longer held the same challenge. He wanted to preach. Monroe, only 25 years old, walked into Dixon's office and resigned because God had called him to preach. Two weeks later, he drove out of Indianapolis, all of his belongings on a Ryder Rental Truck, heading for Columbia, South Carolina.

Bill attended high school in South Carolina, having graduated from Edmunds High School in Sumter where his father pastored Harmony Baptist Church. Monroe knew of the great independent churches up north and in the midwest, but there was no great soul-winning church in South Carolina. He spent three days in Columbia, but couldn't find an apartment to rent. His furniture remained on the rental truck. Pastor David Wood, Harbor Baptist Church, counseled with him and suggested a church was needed on the other side of town. Nothing opened up there, either.

Then, Monroe visited Florence, South Carolina, where an old friend, Larry Denham, lived. They drove around looking at the subdivisions. Florence, a city of 42,000 was quite a mission field with no independent fundamental church. Within an hour, Monroe found a house and a place for his church on the air base. The location was an abandoned theater building, a decaying frame structure with red asbestos brick siding peeling off the walls, that had been used by the Florence Little Theater Association. The interior was painted completely black so no light would reflect.

As Monroe looks back, his first message there was the first sermon he ever preached. He had spoken at other meetings or in Sunday School, but had not preached before beginning. the church. "I just prepared a Sunday School lesson and shouted it," he relates.

The roof leaked, and one time as Monroe preached on baptism during a hard rain, the roof sprang a leak, drenching him with water. During the next two years, the church service was cancelled several times because of rain. According to Monroe, "No one took his coat off that first winter." Two hundred dollars a month spent on fuel oil couldn't keep the building warm. Sunday School was held in a room out back, which was nothing more than tin wrapped around studs in a concrete floor. The ladies stuffed rags in the holes in the nursery wall to keep it warm and had to watch the children carefully lest they rip decaying beaver board off the walls.

When Monroe went into the little theater building, some traditional church men in town made fun of him, accusing him of

Pastor Bill Monroe

Worship Service at Florence Baptist Temple

having "whooping religion" or reviving the Salvation Army. Even though the young congregation had questionable facilities, they had a prediction of success. Dr. Greg Dixon drove down from Indianapolis to preach the organizational sermon; Cecil Hodges presided at the business meeting, and six other pastors were there in May 1970, when the church was chartered. This was the first Baptist Bible Fellowship church in the area. Monroe relies heavily upon the counsel of both Greg Dixon and Cecil Hodges when he has a problem. He simply picks up the phone and seeks their advice on how to build a church, for those who have done it can help him most.

Monroe sold door-to-door products part-time for the first four months to keep his family alive. He testifies, "We ran up all the credit possible on our credit cards; the church just wouldn't go forward." Attendance began with 18 and for two months averaged only 23. Monroe confessed that he was discouraged. When he had been in Florence several months, he discovered that there was a former Independent Baptist church, The Baptist Tabernacle. The former church had split and both sections went into the Southern Baptist Convention. No one seemed to want anything to do with an independent church.

In January, he attended a Georgia-Florida Baptist Bible Fellowship Ministerial where the pastors asked him to appear and tell about his work. After they heard of his vision, they pledged $100 a week to help the new church. Most of the money came from Pastor Cecil Hodges, Bible Baptist Church, Savannah. The pastor came back to Florence, elated. According to him, "I visited with more enthusiasm than ever before."

That March, he had one of his greatest victories; the congregation prayed for 55 in Sunday School. He gave away a "Judas coin" to everyone who came. Monroe testifies, "People kept coming, more than I had ever seen, and we hit 55 that day. It was a real answer to prayer." In May, they went for a goal of 100, giving away goldfish and sponsoring a local quartet; they had 102 in Sunday School. On the church's first anniversary in November, attendance reached 200 for the first time. The young church, with its youthful pastor, was on the march. Still, the church had no capital assets, but were renting the old theater building for $58.50 a month. By this time, they were paying the pastor full time. Monroe signed a note at the bank for $1,100 and bought three old buses. Attendance pushed its way to 140 in Sunday School, a phenomenal growth, judged by the history of the church.

I first heard of Bill Monroe when speaking to a denominational ministers' meeting in Fresno, California. After challenging the men to attempt to "double your attendance," the national president took the pulpit and testified that he had pastored in Florence for approximately ten years and had approximately 100 in attendance for the whole time. "There's a new Independent Baptist Church in Florence that has 200 in Sunday School. They do everything our speaker has told us to do and their building is so bad it is about to fall down.

After Monroe had been in the Church two years he attended the pastor's school at First Baptist Church, Hammond, Indiana, where Dr. Jack Hyles taught him to be bold in leadership, to let the people know where he was going, what he expected and why he had such expectations. He came home to apply the challenge.

Monroe was looking for property all over Florence when a 10-acre tract on South #301 came to his attention. He remembers asking a tenant farmer about the property. The man went inside to phone the owner and Monroe stood on the porch out of the rain, praying for God's will. They agreed upon $50,000 for the land, but Monroe only had $1,000 in the building fund. Immediately the church went into a $200,000 bond sale. Since Monroe had built a solid foundation in the theater building, there was enough income to pay the bonds as they came due. Monroe used his business experience to wisely invest the money raised through selling $200,000 in bonds. The small congregation that had nothing, then needed to buy everything:

Land	$ 50,000
Building & Interest	131,800
Hard Top	5,000
Driveway & Parking Lots	5,000
Illuminated Sign	2,200
Printing Press & Equipment	1,500
Office Equipment	1,500
School Desks & Chalkboards	2,000
	$200,000

The congregation moved into the 15,000 square feet of new facilities on April 9, 1972. Now, they had room for expansion. The new auditorium would seat 500, and the eight classrooms furnished space for the Sunday School to reach 400 average attendance. Only 377 attended Sunday School on the first Sunday they moved into their new building. However, Monroe feels that represented a great victory because there were 32 additions. The community knew that the church was there to stay.

The new facilities on the four-lane highway are located in a pecan orchard that one visitor called "a natural South Carolina landscape." Modern architectural lines attract the visitor. The building is carpeted throughout with wide halls and well-lighted facilities which makes it resemble a modern public school.

After he moved into the facilities, Monroe bought more buses, running the attendance up to 200 on the buses. There is a large sign in the hallway consisting of three columns of statistics: (1) souls sought, (2) souls brought, and (3) souls saved. The first column indicates how many visits were made; second, how many attended Sunday School; and third, those who have accepted Jesus Christ.

When I first visited the church, they were three years old and averaging 400 in Sunday School. I challenged the congregation to have 7,000 in Sunday School and be one of the largest in the world. There was a spontaneous "Amen!" — as if every person in the room expected to build the largest Sunday School in the world right in Florence, South Carolina.

FINANCIAL STABILITY

The Florence Baptist Temple is one of the most financially stable churches in our nation, even though it is only four years old. Many preachers could learn much about financial stability from the Florence Baptist Temple. There are two basic philosophies in church financing. First, management by *assets*. Many church leaders have felt that as long as assets are greater than liabilities, a church can expand through deficit financing. These leaders have gone into excessive bond programs, purchasing more assets (building, property, buses, television equipment), always keeping their total debt under their total worth. As a result, their church has a good financial record on paper, but there is one problem. Many of these churches do not have weekly income to pay off their indebtedness. Some have gotten into bond trouble, having to sell off assets or face the embarrassment of not being able to pay bonds.

The second philosophy is *financing by cash flow*. This approach simply controls the spending so that a church will not obligate itself for more bonds or loans than its weekly offerings can presently liquidate, while at the same time, pay all of its operating expenses. This simple philosophy dictates that a church must have more cash income than outgo.

Monroe has built his church on cash flow. This has resulted in large facilities, respect from the financial community, confidence of the congregation and a sound basis on which to plan future growth. At present, the church has 40,000 square feet of heated-cooled space worth $700,000 with a total indebtedness of $500,-000. Even though a high indebtedness, payments are well within the weekly income of the church. When asked for the secret to financing, the young pastor gave the following guidelines he has followed in developing the financial program of the church.

1. *Don't badger the people for extra money.* Monroe believes in a New Testament principle of tithing and tries to get everyone to tithe. "Not to give the tithe, but pay it." As a result, he doesn't take many extra offerings. Last year, he took one at Christmas for missions and another when they moved into the new building. He notes, "If I wear out my people about money crying 'wolf', they won't believe me when I have a special need." Continuing this argument, Monroe points out that material possessions are always secondary in the Lord's work, but some churches have made it primary. He makes a man's relationship to Jesus Christ the most important ministry of his church. Then, if a man loves God, he will give out of obedience and love. "I don't want people to think giving money is drudgery. It would kill the whole spirit of our church."

2. *Keep finances open.* A quarterly financial report is made to the congregation where all expenses are listed and explained to the congregation. However, staff salaries are not listed individually. Monroe indicates, "I don't think it is right to reveal a staff salary anymore than the other members in the church should reveal what they make." When people have a question about the finances, it is honestly approached and answered.

3. *An annual audited statement.* The business community has

great respect for Florence Baptist Temple because Dal Felkel and Associates, a Certified Public Accounting firm, issues an annual audited statement which means an examination is made to determine the church's integrity and propriety in handling finances. As a result, the people give with confidence because they know an outside authority places its "stamp of approval" upon finances.

4. *Listen to your accountant.* Monroe indicates a young preacher should get good financial advice from the business community. He indicates he doesn't always listen to his accountant, but to go against his accountant is a financial risk. He then indicates that his accountant has been right many more times than the financial advice he has received from fellow pastors or other interested friends in the church. Any new adventure is always based on a feasibility study. Monroe knows what every program costs him; he also has a cost per student in his Florence Christian Schools. As a result, there is never guesswork in starting new programs.

5. *An annual stewardship banquet.* Monroe indicates he learned from Jerry Falwell how to get yearly commitments from his people. A local restaurant is rented, and the people are charged one dollar for a meal that costs approximately three dollars. A good program is planned and a well known speaker is invited to bring the stewardship message. Prior to the banquet, the month of January is dedicated to emphasizing stewardship. Every Sunday School lesson as well as every sermon emphasizes giving money to God. Testimonies are given by laymen of how God has blessed them because they have tithed.

At the stewardship banquet, an audited report is given to every member along with a budget for the coming year. The people see what they can do through tithing. They have seen these buildings, equipment, property and they know that souls walk the aisle each week because they have given sacrificially. "I don't have to beg them to give."

6. *I never look at the giving records.* Monroe doesn't know what his people give financially, indicating he might be adversely influenced by those who gave more or he might judge a rich man who gave less. This way he can deal with everyone on the same basis. He jokingly adds, "I preach hard on tithing as though no one does, and ask for commitments as though everyone will." He

Exterior View of Florence Baptist Temple

warns young preachers that if the people feel the pastor is snooping in the financial records, they won't give.

7. *Giving is the highest form of worship.* Monroe indicates some Baptist preachers make tithing only an obligation. He feels they have degraded tithing, making it similar to paying the electric bill. He preaches that money is time and life. A man sacrifices his strength or time, getting a paycheck in return. This money is a man's life. Monroe teaches his people that they are giving their strength or life back to God when they drop money in the offering plate. He notes, "Tithing is a barter of life. Their time and life is wrapped up in that envelope. Therefore, giving is the highest form of worship and we are giving ourselves back to God."

8. *Excellent financial records.* When the church first began, Monroe installed a bookkeping system from Litton Business Systems throughout the church. Whereas, he could have purchased a small ledger book from a local secretary supply house for less than $5.00, he paid $400 for a complete system of books so the church would have accurate records. A full-time bookkeeper was employed when the church was running 400. Monroe advises a young pastor, "As soon as you can afford a bookkeeper, hire him." Monroe gets a financial report every Monday morning. He is never in the dark about the financial condition of the church.

9. *Cash on hand to operate four weeks.* As I have studied many of the large churches, those I respect the most have cash on hand to operate on a business-like basis. Most of the churches that operate on cash flow have finances spread across several accounts so that if the money does not come in, the church's ministry is not threatened nor will they lose their testimony being unable to pay their bills. This is quite the opposite to some churches who have so extended themselves financially that the preacher has to run to the back of the auditorium to see if the offering is large enough to cover the checks issued last Friday.

Each week, money is deposited into a sinking fund at a local bank to pay the bond coupons as they mature. The sinking fund runs as high as $50,000 at times. Monroe keeps an emergency fund of $22,000 on hand to redeem any bonds where an individual might come and demand an immediate payment. This money belongs to the church and is kept in the emergency fund. Monroe also keeps approximately $5,000 in the general fund with which to operate.

Monroe warns the young preacher that the sinking fund does not belong to the church, but to the bondholders. A church must never touch this money. The emergency fund could be spent, but Monroe keeps it in case the church runs into financial problems.

Monroe notes confidence is built in the church when people can see on paper that the church is solvent. He always reminds his people that their financial stability is what God has done for them.

PASTOR-CHURCH RELATIONSHIP

When Monroe was asked about taking an established pastorate rather than starting a church, he said, "I don't know about taking a church somebody else started—it's like adoption. I'd rather have my own baby and raise it." When asked if he was afraid of failure, Monroe replied, "I had a deep conviction that I could build a church. There was no doubt about the success of the Florence Baptist Temple in my mind." Reflecting on his feelings, he continued, "I did have financial fears. My wife was six months pregnant and I wondered where the money would come from, but I had no doubts about my ability to build a church."

"I feel possessive about my church because I have given it birth. It is hard to separate the church from my thinking and feeling. If someone criticizes my people, that's a criticism of me. When someone calls us arrogant, I am defensive." Monroe explained that he has tried to build pride into his people. "I was proud of this church when we had only 30. I was never ashamed of the old dilapidated theater building. Even in those early days when we had some marginal special music, I was proud of them because they were my people." The church continued to grow because of the deep respect that Monroe had for his congregation. "I never met a rich or dignified person that I couldn't honestly invite to our services."

In further commenting on the charge of being arrogant, Monroe explained, "I believe we are better than any other church in town." The church's growth in money, attendance and attraction of the dignified along with the poor has reinforced Monroe's pride in his church. When asked why he felt Florence Baptist Temple was the best in town, Monroe replied, "(1) Because we have expanded more in money, attendance, and conversions than anyone else in town. The church probably is the fastest growing in the state over the past four years. (2) Because our members are more excited about their church, and they go everywhere telling others what Christ is doing for us. (3) Because we are winning souls through our visitation and bus routes. These are not just children, but adults. I don't see this in other churches in town. (4) Because of our doctrinal and practical soundness. We may not be more correct in doctrine than some Southern Baptist churches, but we are correct in our separation and soul-winning zeal. At the same time, some churches have great zeal but are not growing because they are "off" on some vital doctrines. (Monroe notes that a church can be "as straight as a gun barrel on doctrine" and never grow because it is evangelistically dead.) (5) Because we have an exciting total church program. We try to minister to all of the needs of all of our people. The church has a day care program, Christian school program through eighth grade, Jolly 60's program for the senior citizens, an Awana program to teach Christian character and skills, a daily radio program, plus an extensive counseling ministry."

Whereas, many young churches hope they will succeed, Monroe has a positive mental attitude about success and plans for it (he has success motivation signs around the office area). As an illustration, he comments, "I know souls will come down the aisle because they have been lined up to come forward before the invitation. We have a successful invitation because we plan for it." Someone has received the Lord in every Sunday morning service for three years. Recently, when a man came forward Monroe told the congregation that he had been by this man's home and talked with him, leading him to the Lord. Turning to the wife, Monroe commented how she had prayed faithfully for years for her husband's salvation. Monroe's leadership in soul-winning is one of the keys for the church's growth.

Monroe feels God has put him in the area to build a large church to saturate the entire area. He testifies, "I have followed *Church Aflame* (written by the author and Jerry Falwell) in building the church to minister to the community through a church newspaper, circulation of 3,000), radio, Sunday School buses and organized visitation.

Monroe is known as "the preacher who rebaptizes people." He answers, "When we get church members of another denomination, they must be baptized as a profession of faith in Jesus Christ." He preaches hard against sin and has high standards for his workers and Sunday School teachers. They can't smoke, use alcoholic beverages, dance or attend movies.

Even though the church is young, there is a purity among the members evidenced in other fast-growing churches. A high number of entire families attend the church. Before they were saved, they were members of dead churches. They bring to the church stability. Many in town call Monroe a "Pentecostal Baptist" because of the enthusiastic singing, evangelistic preaching and rebaptizing of church members who are saved in the church.

Monroe confessed that he floundered in the Lord's work before going to work for Indianapolis Baptist Temple because of the interdenominational influence in his life. "Deeper Life" ministry had no appeal to him; but when he met Baptist preachers concerned with soul-winning, building churches, doing something for God, he felt a compelling urge to preach the gospel. His study of the doctrine of the local church led to his call to the ministry.

Monroe accepted Christ at five years of age at his mother's knee. His father had been a preacher in West Virginia; he later moved to South Carolina and now works on his son's staff. He grew up in a parsonage and confesses, "I had an uneventful childhood." He attended the University of South Carolina for three and a half years, a business major, before deciding to go into a quartet ministry, traveling first to Fort Worth, Texas. Later, he became Director of Music for the Indianapolis Baptist Temple.

FUTURE

When Monroe moved into his new facilities, he indicated they would be starting a Christian school the following fall. He began with 75 students—kindergarten through grade three. The following year, enrollment expanded to grade six, with four kindergartens and a total of 225 in school. This year there were 400 enrolled.

Eight full-time workers staff the young church. The Florence Christian Schools have a staff of 22.

Three years ago, the church had a $26,000 income; two years ago, the budget reached $62,717. This past year, the church received $233,987.61 in its church and school. This year, the total income will pass $400,000. Only a small percentage of churches in America have a larger cash flow.

Monroe feels the church will be averaging 1,200 in Sunday School before the fifth anniversary. This is not a visionary goal, but a real possibility.

CHAPTER TEN

A "SWEET, SWEET SPIRIT" COMES OUT OF A CHURCH SPLIT

FELLOWSHIP BAPTIST CHURCH
Huntington, West Virginia
FRED V. BREWER, *Pastor*

Those who split churches are often slammed for being schismatic and contentious, but the founding of Fellowship Baptist Church, Huntington, West Virginia, is a story of a "sweet, sweet spirit." The rapid expansion of the new church, doubling its attendance and reaching an attendance of 1,009 on the first anniversary, is evidence that God can be glorified when brethren disagree.

Pastor Fred V. Brewer knew God had called him to the city of Huntington in the tri-state corner of the Ohio River Valley. But he had difficulty understanding the turn of events leading to his resignation at Highlawn Baptist Church after only 18 months, especially since he had baptized 105 converts during a three-week period just a month before his resignation.

The Highlawn Baptist Church was searching for a pastor in 1970 when a member toured the Holy Land with Cecil Hodges, Pastor of the Bible Baptist Church, Savannah, Georgia. Hodges recommended Fred Brewer, who was returning from a special mission project in Hawaii. At that time, Highlawn was the largest American Baptist Convention church in West Virginia. The church leaders assured Brewer that they wanted to become an independent church. To prove this, they cited the fact that a committee had been formed to study withdrawal from the American Baptist Convention, but the deacons voted to defer a recommendation because

106

the church had no pastor. Highlawn was conservative in doctrine. had led the Convention one year in baptisms and had designated its funds only for missions at the national level. Also, Highlawn did not use Convention Sunday School literature and had filed a letter of protest against the National Council of Churches at the denominational office.

The pulpit committee arranged for Brewer to preach at another church in the Huntington area, where they heard him and recommended him as an official candidate. He was voted in with a larger than 95 percent vote.

According to Brewer, "A crisis of leadership was inevitable; the church was organized according to the suggested denominational structure, with a number of powerful committees. An aggressive pastor would rock the boat." Brewer brought renewed outreach to the Highlawn Church which reached a high of 893 that first year on "Old Fashioned Day," celebrated in conjunction with Huntington's centennial celebration. Next, 1,223 attended Sunday School on "Friend Day," an all-time attendance record for the church. Prior to Brewer's coming, the church had been going down in attendance for twelve years.

In the spring of 1971, the author visited the church and, at the request of the deacons, wrote an appraisal of the church. I evaluated it as a "committee-bound" church. The report was resented by the lay leaders but focused attention on the struggle for leadership in the church. The controversy did not arise over theology nor the American Baptist Convention, but over leadership. When 105 were baptized within three weeks, a deacon said, "We aren't opposed to those being saved, but with so many coming into the church, we will lose control of our church." Strangely, the confrontation came, not because of any wrong action by Brewer, but due to the supposed threat the "power-structure" felt over the rapid growth.

Brewer said he was faced with the alternative. "If I had brought the vote to a showdown, I could have gotten the majority and would have gotten the buildings, but underlying problems would have remained in the church." He went on, "We would have had squabbles for several years and because of fighting, lost our testimony." He testified, "We forsook the building to gain the city!"

At a deacons' meeting on June 7, 1972, they asked for his resignation. Brewer replied the next day to the chairman. "The deacons

Exterior View of Fellowship Baptist Church

didn't call me and the deacons can't dismiss me. This is a Baptist church and I am responsible to the people." He read his resignation to the congregation the following Sunday morning. After the evening service, a friendly reception was held for him at the local Holiday Inn with 250 attending.

While the undercurrent of opposition to pastoral leadership was growing, a second tide was swelling. Many members were dissatisfied with the ecclesiastical hierarchy in the church. Herman Moore, a sincere and dedicated deacon with a spiritual concern, felt the undercurrent and asked to sponsor a prayer meeting for unity in the church. This was granted, and the week before Brewer's resignation, 100 people gathered to pray for harmony. Up until then, there was no thought of a new church. Brewer knew that he was going to leave, so he counseled the group meeting with Moore to resolve their differences with the deacons.

"The deacons wouldn't listen to us, but treated us like children," said Moore. Looking back, Brewer testifies that Moore was raised up by God to bring the new church into existence. Moore observed, "We couldn't understand the trouble in the church; people were walking the aisle and we wanted revival to continue."

After Brewer resigned on Sunday, a prayer meeting for Wednesday was planned. A telephone committee was quickly organized, and 100 families were called in 30 minutes. The meeting was held at the YWCA building with 229 attending and Brewer and Moore presiding. The group was much larger than the deacons of the old church had anticipated. The Brewers left on Friday to join 11 young people from the group who were already in Mexico with SMITE (Summer Missionary Intern Training for Evangelism). Men within the group spoke for the congregation's first meeting on Sunday. When the Brewers returned from Mexico the following Friday, a crowd of 150 met them at the airport. They journeyed in car caravan to a nearby church where they had a gospel meeting, Brewer testifying of the ministry in Mexico. A young married man was saved as the invitation was given. The congregation remained upstairs, while Moore and five men went downstairs to talk with Brewer about being the new pastor. Brewer told them, "You don't want me—I'll be a stumbling block to you. I'll have the reputation of being a church-splitter."

"We had a meeting last night with the heads of families to

discuss finances and salary," the men told Brewer. "We are confident that it is the Lord's will for you to be our pastor."

"We've issued a call to Fred Brewer and he has accepted," announced Moore to the waiting congregation. Shouts of "Amen!" and applause reverberated through the building. Brewer told the people, "I tried not to lead a split, as you know, but it is evident that the Lord is in this. If love and unity can be used to build a church, we will have the greatest church in the tri-state area."

Moore described the exodus: "We walked away gently." There was never a meeting with an ugly scene or a mass resignation. Every new member in Fellowship Baptist Church was accepted on the basis of faith; they were not voted in as a mass. When Brewer resigned Highlawn, many others resigned privately (not in a mass meeting). Brewer points out, "They were going to leave, whether or not I became their pastor. These people were independent minded and could no longer accept the spiritually stifling 'power-structure.' Today our church is not denominationally affiliated in any way."

Immediately, a committee was formed to choose a name. They had to write checks and become an organized body. Thirty names were reduced to two—*Fellowship and Trinity*. Since "fellowship" was the message of the church, they unanimously decided on "Fellowship Baptist Church," voting on the name while Brewer was in Mexico.

The young congregation met in 11 different locations for the next 57 services, including Ritter City Park, gymnasiums, the YMCA and YWCA buildings, and other churches. Several times the people went home without knowing where they could meet for the next service. The phone committee stayed busy just keeping the congregation knit together.

The congregation visited two churches to consider purchase, but the buildings were too small at their first meetings. Brewer testifies, "The barnacles dropped off during those three months without a building. Some of these people had spent their life in High-lawn Baptist Church, and many left relatives as well as close friends there. As they moved from one temporary site to another, they lost their preconception of traditional Christianity. They exercised real faith for the first time, and were made willing to trust and follow the Lord." Brewer preached on the New Testament church during those days. To show their commitment to the Great Commission, before they had even secured property, they bought a bus and named it "Genesis." Later, the second bus was named "Exodus" and the next two were "Matthew" and "Mark."

At their first meetings, the congregation remembered hearing Jerry Wayne Bernard sing "There's a Sweet, Sweet Spirit" at their spring revival. The infant congregation sang it once, and it so warmed their spirits that they have sung it at every meeting since. From the beginning Brewer admonished his people to keep this "sweet spirit" and to guard against even the slightest bitterness, since many harsh and untrue statements had been made against them. Bernard's recording of the song is used on the church's weekday radio program, "Fellowship With The Word." Today, they call themselves "The church with the sweet, sweet spirit."

Even though the majority of the people came from Highlawn, charter members came from 16 other churches. Those who joined from other churches knew of the revival at Highlawn and wanted to become part of a great super-aggressive church that had the right motives, the right spiritual attitude and willingness to obey clear biblical instructions.

The founding service was led by G.B. Vick, Temple Baptist Church, Detroit, on July 21, 1972. Brewer read the preamble from the by-laws and asked all 306 charter members to sign. Being then constituted, they ratified the previous actions, Articles of Faith and the calling of a pastor. Then they elected trustees to act as their legal representatives and appointed a church clerk and treasurer. According to Brewer, Vick preached one of the greatest sermons of his life, entitled, "These Things We Believe." Dr. Vick told the young congregation, "I have never been with a more exciting church. Your spirit is positively electrifying."

The leadership had a metal building in mind that could be constructed within 60 days. The building committee asked every member to look for property. Brewer testified that he and the committee knew the price and location of every available piece of property in the city. The building committee held over 50 meetings, and its 17 members literally exhausted themselves searching for a permanent location.

At first, the Hullabaloo Dance Hall was turned down. Its 3.5 acres of ground was considered too small, and the psychedelic

The Staff of Fellowship Baptist, l. to r. Fred Brewer, Pastor; Jim Hensley, Youth Pastor; Mac Brake, Bus Pastor; Jim Hedger, Music Director.

Groundbreaking for Sunday School Building, February 11, 1972

decorations on the inside were atrocious. The second time someone suggested the dance hall, the committee became excited after they examined it with the owner on a Sunday afternoon. During the evening services, Brewer reported on the dance hall, and 99 percent of the congregation went to tramp through the weeds that night to scrutinize the hall.

Brewer, feeling the people's excitement, turned to Moore and said, "Our church has just found a home."

They got permission to use the building before a contract was signed and held a prayer meeting there the following Wednesday. Brewer preached from the stand formerly used by go-go dancers. They had secured a bank commitment for a loan if the congregation could raise $25,000 down payment. They had $10,000 in the building fund.

"Get scratch paper and pass it to the people to make commitments," Brewer instructed the ushers that first evening. They added up the pledges in front of the congregation; the total came to $15,000. They had their down payment!

In the regular Wednesday evening offering that night, $6,600 was received. Unknown to the leadership, people had come prepared with money to buy the building, even before it was voted on. Since they got more than they needed, they paid $30,000 down. Three months later, they borrowed a second $100,000 to build Sunday School classrooms.

A Christian contractor suggested the cost could be reduced by $8,000 if they did some of the actual labor. When the building was finished, the men's hard work had saved $20,000. They did all of the painting, plumbing and electrical work. The men worked feverishly to get the building ready for their first anniversary dedication, toiling nearly every night. The ladies provided food and refreshments, working alongside their men.

During construction, visitation continued under direction of Rev. Don Pottorff, the full-time associate, hired when the church was six months old. Also, every Saturday morning the bus workers were visiting.

Brewer announced, "We'll not work all Saturday night before dedication because we'll be so exhausted we can't enjoy this first anniversary." They quit at 7 P.M. and went home to get ready for Sunday.

The pastor had a surprise waiting for them in the parking lot the next morning. A massive multi-colored billboard greeted them on that first anniversary: "Phase Three — Auditorium to seat 1,500 people — Groundbreaking June 9, 1974." A beautiful building similar to that of Temple Baptist Church in Detroit was painted on the sign.

The only outside speaker that day was Vernon Brewer, Youth Minister of Thomas Road Baptist Church, Lynchburg, Virginia, son of Fred Brewer. The congregation had set an attendance goal of 1,000 for its first anniversary. One thousand and nine attended that day, including 222 people on the three buses and two vans. Special guests included West Virginia Secretary of State Edgar Heiskell, the former mayor of Huntington, and the mayor of the adjacent village, Barboursville. When asked how they reached this unusually high number for a church's first anniversary, Brewer remarked, "We didn't use any gimmicks and special attractions other than our first anniversary and building dedication. Our people just worked hard and brought them in."

The local newspaper commented, "The huge ballroom's psychedelic walls and black ceiling has given way to a room full of chairs, walls of cherry paneling and white ceiling garnished with a giant rustic brown cross . . . tiny stages for go-go girls now form the base for a cross-shaped pulpit." The paper went on, "A group of Baptists have literally converted a dance hall from a place of entertainment to a house of worship." The newspaper also described the Phase II Sunday School Unit which includes three large Sunday School departments, a fully equipped kitchen, restrooms with showers, a gymnasium with several uses as a fellowship hall, dining room activities, etc. The groundbreaking for this unit in February featured Brewer and the deacons starting things off by pulling a plow instead of the traditional turning of earth with a shovel. "We decided to use a big plow which characterizes our church with its united teamwork and spirit," remarked Brewer.

The church was missionary-minded from the beginning, sending financial support to *every* independent Baptist missionary who has gone out from their county to the field, including those who have gone from other independent Baptist churches in the area. Brewer commented, "If God raised him up from our area, we ought to support him." More than 10 percent of their income has gone for foreign missions the first year.

Fred Brewer was born in Fort Worth, Texas, 1925, and as a baby was placed in the nursery in the First Baptist Church, where he grew up under the ministry of the legendary J. Frank Norris. His mother and father had been baptized there and taught Sunday School under G. B. Vick, then Sunday School Superintendent. At age 14, young Brewer accepted Jesus Christ. He doesn't know why he put the decision off so long, but attributes his salvation to the influence of two Sunday School teachers, Sam Jones and Horace Ledbetter. Fred usually sat in the rear of the auditorium; he had to walk down the full length of an aisle one city block long. When baptizing the boy, the pastor said, "God bless these tears."

Two years later, young Fred definitely felt God was leading him into the ministry. He went forward during a service to surrender for full-time Christian service. The pastor phoned and left word with the boy's parents to tell young Fred to come by his office on

Dedication of Phase II Sunday School Building

Pastor Fred V. Brewer

the way to Sunday School. There he said, "Young man, if God has laid his hand upon you for the ministry, eat it up, let it devour you." Brewer has tried to let that admonition rule his life.

He graduated from Texas Wesleyan College and also Southwestern Baptist Theological Seminary, both in Fort Worth, and helped to found the Gideon Baptist Church of that city. Later, he enlisted in the army, serving in Korea during the Second World War, and was discharged as a First Sergeant. Brewer also pastored Calvary Baptist Church, Denton, Texas; Lamar Baptist Church, Greenville, Texas; and Park Hill Baptist Church, Pueblo, Colorado, a church that grew from 500 to 1,032 and sent 26 young people into full-time Christian service. Brewer served as a director of the Baptist Bible Fellowship and also on the Missions Committee; and accepted the assignment of a special missions project to pastor the Fellowship Baptist Tabernacle in Honolulu, Hawaii, which grew from 100 to 551 in 28 months. When Brewer left Hawaii, he came to Huntington.

Whereas many independent Baptist churches have no committees, Brewer had allowed the formation of a number of committees in the church. He affirms, "Leadership is not what I can do myself, but what I can get others to do." He feels that a strong church is an involved church. When answering the charge of dictatorship, he comments, "There is no difference between a one-man dictatorship (which might be evident in an independent church) or a five-man dictatorship (a church controlled by deacons).

"This church is the most thrilling adventure in my life," noted Brewer. "I can see my people growing together in unity every week. I can see individuals becoming more spiritual under the liberty of the Spirit and their willingness to work."

During the first month of the Fellowship Baptist Church, attendance averaged 241. In its twelfth month, the attendance averaged 420 (not including the record attendance on anniversary Sunday), a 74 percent increase. There were 224 additions in the first year, 109 by baptism. The young congregation has 19 mission outlets, local and worldwide. The first year, it received $132,146, and at present is receiving approximately $2,500 a week income. Today the church is worth $300,000 in capital assets, of which more than one-half has been paid. A youth minister is being added to the church staff, and six more buses will be added during the year.

From the beginning, the church has reflected a full-grown maturity of dedicated Christians who could pray and love. These members are grounded in the Word of God, tithe, and delight to see souls saved. This solid base promises future growth.

CHAPTER ELEVEN

THE FASTEST GROWING CHURCH IN RICHMOND

OPEN DOOR BAPTIST CHURCH
Richmond, Virginia
DANNY SMITH, *Pastor*

The Open Door Baptist Church which advertises itself as "The Fastest Growing Church in Richmond," was begun by a young man, Danny Smith, who might be considered too young to pastor a flock. However, the rapid growth to an average of over 743 in four years has proved that God called him to this city of one-half million population to found a super-aggressive church.

The church's history precedes its first meeting on August 10, 1970. It was born of a college student's vision and desire to build a church. Although the church began in the heart of Danny Smith, it doesn't have a human foundation. Just as Danny has built his personal life on Christ, so the Open Door Baptist Church is built on Christ.

Danny Smith was not reared in a Christian home. Tragedy brought two members of the Smith family to Jesus Christ. Danny's older brother, Lewis, crashed his motorcycle head-on into an automobile on a highway near Lynchburg. As he lay on the side of the road, bleeding from head to foot, sure he was dying, he prayed for salvation. Although Lewis was not attending church, he knew enough about the gospel to repent and believe.

G.D. Smith, the boy's father, couldn't believe his eyes when he saw the mangled body of his son on the operating table in Lynchburg General Hospital. Lewis, a football player, had been a perfect

118

specimen of young manhood. The bald father paced the dimly lit halls of the hospital, praying, "Oh God . . .," but the prayers bounced off the walls. He had on many previous occasions promised God to quit his hell-bent ways—but he had broken every promise. Danny's father owned the G.D. Smith Lumber Company and the Virginia Appalachian Lumber Corporation. He had never faced a problem that money and position couldn't solve. But as Lewis lingered near death for two weeks, one night in the halls of the hospital the successful businessman realized he was a sinner and cried for mercy. He made no promises; he only accepted God's Word and pleaded for God's grace. He remembered Jerry Falwell's visits to their home; the family had watched the Thomas Road Church services over television and they received *Word of Life*, the church newspaper. The following Sunday, the father went forward in the church, rededicating his life to Jesus Christ. Lewis recovered and became a member of Thomas Road.

In June 1965, Danny's father took him to a revival at Thomas Road to hear Dr. J. Harold Smith. After the service, the father introduced the high school junior to the evangelist. J. Harold Smith, known for his great pulpit oratory, took his Bible that Thursday evening and showed Danny how to be saved. The two knelt at the front bench in the auditorium where Danny received Jesus Christ as Saviour. The following Sunday, Jerry Falwell baptized him and he immediately became involved in the work of the church. That fall he was elected President of the Youth Department. The testimony of Rudy Holland, saved three months earlier, made a deep impact on his life. (The boys were later to become great friends.)

Danny had made poor marks in school for 11 years, but after salvation he began to study and apply himself, with resultant improvement in grades. He attempted to win his school friends to the Lord. One day after baseball practice, Danny told the coach, "I have something to say to the team." Since Danny was first string catcher, he got permission. After sitting the buddies down, he "preached" to them and gave an invitation; five or six received Christ.

Two years before his college graduation, Danny Smith worked as visitation pastor for Thomas Road Baptist Church and often talked with Jerry Falwell about starting a church in Virginia. Fal-

Pastor Danny Smith

well stated, "If I were a young man, I'd go to Richmond, the largest city in Virginia." Smith graduated from Tennessee Temple Schools, Chattanooga, Tennessee, in 1970. He visited Richmond three times between May and July, looking over the city. Each time, God gave him a burden for the extensive suburbs stretching over the pine hills of the city. There was no great fundamental church on the west side. Though he tried several times to start a church there, God opened doors on the south side of the city.

Danny met Mrs. Booker in Lynchburg. Her home was Richmond. When she learned Smith planned to build a church like Thomas Road in her town, she vowed to help the young man get started.

Smith talked to the school board, but they refused his request to rent a school. Next, he talked with a Christian school about using their facilities, but his request bogged down in board meetings. He determined, "If I have to preach on the street corner, I'm starting a church in Richmond." Smith moved his mobile home to Richmond in August, locating in Dodd's Trailer Park. On Wednesday night, Jerry Falwell took up a $300 love offering to help pay Smith's living expenses in Richmond. Smith left on Thursday.

Mrs. Booker sent Danny to see Garland Dodds, who helped him obtain use of the Volunteer Fire Department in Chester, near Richmond. The group met in a large upstairs open room. Eight gathered that first Sunday, August 10, 1970: Danny Smith and his wife, Gail; Mr. and Mrs. Booker and their son, Bobby; Mr. and Mrs. Vaughn and child. The first Sunday the church received $90 in offerings that went to pay for expenses and a small salary for Smith. Next Sunday 33 people met at the Manchester Community Center which Smith had arranged to rent for $100 a month. The facilities included a large room that could seat 200, along with three classrooms.

During the first week of September, Jerry Falwell conducted an evangelistic crusade each evening at the community center, preaching the gospel; several received the Lord. On the last night of the crusade, September 5, Falwell organized the church with 33 charter members.

That evening they elected a treasurer and church clerk, with three trustees to hold the property for the congregation. Smith indicated, "We waited one year before electing deacons bcause we were not sure of the maturity of the men in the congregation." Young Pastor Smith recommends that all churches proceed slowly in electing deacons, as he did.

The church grew rapidly; by November, it averaged 100 in Sunday School. Within six months, Danny Smith went on the radio, preaching Monday through Friday. His new converts joined with him in completely covering the area by visitation, inviting residents to Sunday School, attempting to lead them to Christ.

That first 18 months in rented facilities were difficult. At first, Danny set up chairs and took them down again Sunday evening. His wife kept the nursery, and he was responsible for a host of small details. Within six months the men began helping, so Smith could give more time to greeting visitors and members of his young congregation. When they finally moved into their own building, he testified, "I was never so glad to get into a building in all my life."

In the eighth month of their existence, the church had a missionary conference and voted to contribute to the support of 18 missionaries. Today, they help support 21 missionaries on a monthly basis. Smith comments, "God has blessed us for that commitment to reach the world."

The church received a total of $27,000 in its first year. Immediately, Smith planned a stewardship banquet to receive faith promises for the second year. Before the banquet, the Sunday School lesson emphasized tithing, Smith preached sacrificial giving, and Jerry Falwell spoke at the stewardship banquet at a local restaurant. Members pledged $37,000 for the second year but actually took in $60,000. The third year, the members pledged $57,000 at the stewardship banquet and received a total of $110,000. Reflecting the practice of most Baptist churches, half of the church income is usually pledged at the annual stewardship banquet.

While the church was meeting in the community center and looking for property, Smith placed $1,000 in escrow on ten acres of ground on Hull Street Road. The church was assured the ground would be adequate for a septic tank sewerage system; however, the property failed to pass public health inspection (it wouldn't percolate). The young congregation lost the $1,000.

Smith told Clyde Coleman, treasurer of the community center, how they lost the land. Coleman was sympathetic and said, "I've got some land I want to sell." In conjunction with three neighbors, he owned eight and one-half acres on Orcutt Lane. The group had discussed selling it as a unit and wanted $41,000 for the total plot of ground. After Smith concluded the deal, he learned that the previous ten acres would not have the road frontage he had been promised. Besides, that acreage would have cost $20,000 more than their present site. Smith feels God providentially guided them to the land they now own.

Immediately after purchasing the ground, the church issued $120,000 in bonds and began constructing its first building, with an auditorium to seat 385, and nine classrooms. Smith felt he could average 200 pupils in Sunday School in the first wing. The congregation occupied the building in July, 1971.

The first person saved in the new facilities was Danny's brother, Jimmy Smith. The family had prayed seven years for Jimmy's salvation. He had been in several automobile accidents. His rebellion against God made him a "hard case." But Jimmy's great need made him a candidate for salvation. The new building was only a shell with a roof and sub-floor, but the congregation got a city permit to occupy it for evangelistic meetings. Rodney Bell preached Monday through Saturday. Sunday evening after the revival, Danny preached on "He Reached Down His Hand for Me." He testified, "Jimmy is the only one in the family who has not made a profession of faith." Jimmy sat in the second row, his little boy asleep in his arms. As the Gethsemane Quartet sang the invitation, Danny thought, "The baby in his arms makes it too hard for Jimmy to come forward." As the quartet continued singing, Jimmy stood up blurted, "Danny, I can't wait any longer!" With his little boy in his arms, he walked through folded chairs, knocking some to the floor. With the baby still in his arms, he fell at the altar where Danny led him to the Lord.

Two hundred and ninety people attended the dedication of the new building where Falwell spoke; a month later, 602 attended their second anniversary. The Gethsemane Quartet (Greensboro, North Carolina) sang, and the congregation had dinner on the grounds. By this time, the church was running five buses and was optimistic about growth and expansion. On Harvest Day, 1972 (Thanksgiving), the church reached 790, with 348 riding the five buses.

The first bond issue of $120,000 took one year to sell, discouraging Danny Smith. In January, 1973, he prepared to sell a second issue. The church adopted the slogan "Over the top without a stop — All the way in one day." Young Danny was determined to sell every bond immediately. On Sunday, February 25, 1973, the trained workers began taking orders on the issue. The committee had been lining up prospects for three weeks, getting commitments. People began reserving bonds on Sunday morning. Danny Smith, along with Ben Bates of Ambassador Church Finances, vowed he wouldn't eat until every bond was sold — a dangerous threat in light of previous lagging sales. On Sunday evening, the church still had $37,000 worth of uncommitted bonds. During the evening service, every bond was committed and the two men went out to "get the biggest steak in Richmond." Young Smith testified, "Selling those bonds showed me that nothing is impossible in God's service." He felt revival begin to surge through the church as a result of successfully selling the bonds.

The church never borrowed money for its buses; the money was raised in the services. The first bus cost $500 and was purchased from Jerry Falwell. Smith told the people he had a burden to reach the lost through buses. He asked for volunteers to stand up and make a financial commitment to purchase a bus. He got two promises of $100; the rest came in $20 and $10 pledges. He painted his bus blue and white. Later, three more buses were purchased. John Wells, a young convert, borrowed $600 to purchase one of the three. According to Smith, this was amazing, inasmuch as Wells had only an average job.

Danny knows God answers prayer; he exhorts other beginning pastors to trust God for finances. Early in the church's existence, they owed $4,000. Until that time, the only way money came in was through the offering plate. Two banks had refused him a $4,000 loan. Danny asked the people to pray for a miracle, and when one man sold his home in Florida, he sent $2,000 to the church. A few days later, they received a second check for $2,000 in the mail. He affirmed, "That proved to me God is able to provide our needs if we pray and believe."

God has provided for Smith's family needs in miraculous ways. Two of the Smith children were born in Richmond, but Danny did not have hospitalization. A friend donated a $2,000 church bond to pay off the hospital and doctor bills.

The church began advertising on television with five spot announcements each weekend. Danny Smith began, "If you were to die in the next 30 minutes, where would you spend eternity?" During the Friday night movie, this was a startling question to confront a man with a can of beer or a housewife who had just settled the kids down for sleep. In each commercial, Smith quotes Scripture and tells about the church. The commercials have made the church's location on Orcutt Lane well known throughout the city.

Billboards on the sides of city buses advertise the church's existence. Also, a huge billboard on the Jefferson Davis Highway, at the corner of U.S. 301 and Route 1, inform the city of the ministry of the Open Door Baptist Church. Bumper stickers advertise: "There is a difference. Come and see." Weekly newspaper ads and a monthly church paper are used. At present, 4,200 people are on the mailing list.

During its third year, the church sponsored "The Open Door Bible Institute." Harold Willmington, Dean, Thomas Road Bible Institute, came each Monday evening and taught the Bible to 185 laymen from the Open Door Church and other churches in Greater

Richmond. This weekly teaching of the Bible strengthened the number of new Christians, stabilizing the church for future growth.

Smith felt money should be invested in evangelism rather than in beautiful buildings, so he has hired full-time personnel to reach people. In January, 1973, he hired his first secretary, Mrs. Charlsie Long. Two months later, Jim Sandefur, a full-time Lynchburg Baptist College student, became part-time music and youth director. In July, 1973, Marvin Layne was hired as director of buses. During the spring campaign in 1973, the Sunday School averaged 557. On its third anniversary the church reached 905 in Sunday School; 482 rode the ten buses. Record attendance was set on B-7 Sunday in March 1974 with 1,414 in attendance.

Evangelist J.O. Grooms came to work for the church in September, 1973 as director of soul-winning. Grooms initiated the workable idea of "soul-winning tours," where a leader of a church takes two laymen with him to observe soul-winning in action. Pastor Smith, Grooms, and Marvin Layne lead the tours and laymen sign up to observe personal evangelism in action at one of three different periods: 10 to 12 A.M.; 2 to 4 P.M.; and 7 to 9 P.M. The observers do not talk, they just listen. According to Grooms, "The law of the Medes and Persians is in operation; every person must come or get a substitute to take his place."

During a recent testimony meeting, several adults jumped to witness to their enthusiasm and growth as they watched their staff members deal with lost people. One testified he was afraid and came only as an observer. An unexpected advantage of soul-winning tours is that they force church leaders into the homes of the lost. The added pressure of the observing laymen motivates them to be more diligent in persuading the lost to receive the Lord.

The church has been built through soul-winning rather than attracting disgruntled members from other churches. "We have had few people walking the aisle, bringing their letters with them," states Danny Smith.

In the fall of 1973, the young pastor witnessed to John McQuire, but he was hardened to the gospel and cut the conversation short. Even Mrs. McQuire couldn't get her husband to visit Sunday School. When a close friend of McQuire's was shot and killed, his self-confidence was shaken. Danny led McQuire to the

Open Door Baptist Church

Lord in his home early one Tuesday morning. John McQuire was baptized immediately and began serving in the church.

Ralph Smith visited the church and got mad at the preaching, saying he would never come back. John McQuire heard Ralph's complaints and asked the young preacher to go talk with Ralph who received the Lord and is now a faithful bus captain.

On another occasion Danny Smith met Earl West, who seemed interested in the gospel but was unresponsive. Danny returned six or seven times before Earl West knelt by the couch to receive the Lord. He is now a bus captain and has had a record of 108 on his bus.

Seven-year-old Buddy Qualls attended Sunday School and received Jesus Christ as his Saviour. No one in the church doubted his salvation although the boy was young. He had been having dizzy spells. Doctors diagnosed his malady as a brain tumor. They operated, but the tumor was too deep and everyone began preparing for his inevitable death. Danny Smith visited in the hospital and asked the boy, "Who's in your heart?" Buddy said, "Jesus!"

Buddy's birthday was in May, but everyone knew he wouldn't live past March. A giant birthday party was planned for him and the local newspapers gave it full coverage. Bozo the clown and newsmen were there. Buddy was given a soldier's suit like the men wore at Fort Lee, Virginia, and the color guard made him an honorary sergeant in the army. Buddy's red hair and freckles, which had captured the heart of the church, were seen by newspapers throughout the city.

Little Buddy was buried in his soldier's outfit. Danny admitted shamelessly, "I openly wept at the funeral. While preaching the sermon, I had to struggle to keep from breaking down completely." Through the church's Sunday School other little boys will be reached with the gospel of Christ.

CHAPTER TWELVE

GETTING OFF ON THE RIGHT FOOT

PRINCIPLES OF FOUNDING A CHURCH

Is there a formula for starting a church? Some young men look for the perfect plan to begin a church, thinking if they have the successful blueprint, they can't fail. To ask for a pattern for starting a church is like asking for a pattern for wrestling an alligator. The "critter" is so slippery and dangerous that the best advice is, "Don't get killed."

Starting a church has many variables. Neighborhoods are different (inner-city, rural, racially mixed, upper-class, etc.); people are different (spiritually mature, uneducated, new babes in Christ, etc.); and pastor-planters have different strengths (evangelistic, Bible teacher, counselor, musical, etc.). Therefore, there seems to be a different way to wrestle each alligator. But, out of the churches described in this book, there emerges a skeleton outline for getting started right. The following points are suggested to guide a new pastor-planter. However, he should be warned: (1) Not every point applies in every situation; and (2) other principles not suggested in this book will have to be employed. This manuscript is not exhaustive due to its pioneering effort and lack of capacity to survey all newly started works. The points in this chapter are illustrated in the ten previous case studies.

I. THE RIGHT DIRECTION

The most important factor in beginning a church is its conception in the mind of God's man who is motivated by the Holy Spirit.

I said in *The Ten Largest Sunday Schools* (Baker Book House, 1969), "The church was large in the heart of the pastor long before it was large on the street corner." This is true of beginning churches as well as of massive congregations.

The foundation of a New Testament church requires a man called of God. If a man is going to start a successful church, he must be fully confident that God has led him to do so. The heartaches, pressures and hard work required in starting a church demand that the pastor have the assurance of the call of God. Rudy Holland testifies, "I remember many times when quitting would have been so easy. The assurance that God was going to do something in the Roanoke Valley through the Berean Baptist Church compelled me to keep pressing forward."

Danny Smith agreed: "I had a definite conviction that beginning Open Door Baptist Church was God's call to me." Perry Purtle adds, "I was absolutely sure it was God's will" (Heb. 11:1).

First, the spiritual authority is determined: "All power is given unto me . . . go ye" (Matt. 28:18, 19). Next, the correct message is necessary. In days of compromise, people are looking for churches that preach the old-time gospel. The preaching of the Word of God is still the greatest enticement to get people into the house of God. Rudy Holland states, "I am convinced that every growing church must have a positive message. The Word of God gives a positive message, not only to the sinner but to the saint as well." The men in this book, as well as those in my previous books who build successful churches, are committed to the fundamentals of the faith. They believe a message from God is the only hope for a lost, dying, hell-bound humanity. Therefore, they uphold the Bible as the authority for preaching and teaching. God's Word is the foundation of their churches.

After establishing a clear-cut biblical philosophy, these men began ministering out of a predetermined strategy. Perry Purtle reported, "I mapped out a clear-cut strategy and philosophy as to how I felt God wanted this church built. I immediately began to set goals (long-and short-range goals). This simple formula we follow: *Plan — Organize — Execute — Control*." (See Chapter Five for description of his plans.)

Here the question is raised, "Should only a man of pastoral experience begin a church, or can a young man out of college be successful?" This question has no clear answer. Jim Singleton and Fred Brewer began churches when past age 40; they had gained experience by serving previous pastorates. Danny Smith, George Zarias, Bud Calvert and Rudy Holland went straight from college to begin a church. The answer lies not in age "or experience, but in strategy. All these men had a preconceived idea of how they would begin a church. This formula gave them confidence in proceeding.

Some of these men set goals of how many members they would have at the end of the first year, because an attendance objective drove them to diligent work. Others knew they would work with every ounce of strength; they didn't need goals. Alden Laird began a new work in North Denver in the fall of 1973 but quickly dropped the numerical goals he had set, testifying, "I have so many young Christians to look after and the church is so thrilling, I don't need goals to drive me. If I feed these young babes in Christ, numbers will take of themselves."

II. GETTING KNOWN

"Seek to become known," advises Rudy Holland. "Advertise. Let people know you are there and state what you believe. People go where they know to go. I recommend starting a radio program as soon as possible in the ministry of any new church. The newspaper, television, and billboard can be used to attract attention to your church. Remember, every successful business is built upon the fact that is has appealed to the market. The church must do the same without compromising the message." However, the young pastor counsels, "Many people have visited our church as a result of advertising, but I know of none who have joined as a result of the advertisements. Advertising will create questions in the minds of the public, but only personal contact will give the answers."

The following list is suggestive for the pioneer pastor. Back of these principles is the concept of saturation evangelism: "Reaching every available person by every available means at every available time." [1]

    1. Get names of prospects (find every available person).
        a. Address of friends and relatives
        b. Newcomers' list

---

[1] Elmer Towns, Jerry Falwell, *Church Aflame*. Nashville: Impact Books, 1971. See Chapter Four for a full discussion of saturation evangelism.

    c. Former high school acquaintances (if pastor is returning to hometown)

    d. Names of unchurched friends given by people in other churches

    e. Community canvass

2. Get brochures and flyers printed immediately. They should include information on the pastor, the doctrine of the church and the type of program the church will offer. Order early, for printing requires time. (Carl Godwin had 3,000 printed, handed out 2,000 and mailed 400.) Mail a personal letter with the flyer.

3. Get a nonprofit permit number from main post office (about 1.7¢ per letter); make sure it's not a permit which requires stamps. Zip codes are essential for bulk mailing.

4. Have pastor's photograph made to use in publicity.

5. Place an ad in local paper, including photo. Give details for first service.

6. Write a press release for the local papers. Take it rather than mail it to the church editors.

7. Contact friends. Godwin kidded his friends about not heckling them in the first service.

8. Begin door-to-door visitation in the area your building is located and tell people the date you will begin services. Invite them to attend.

9. Announce the opening service on the local radio stations. (Usually they will make announcements as a community service, without cost to you.)

10. Use every available means to get the gospel to every available person: television, radio, billboards, newspaper, buses, bumper stickers, etc.

11. Adopt a good slogan for your church. Danny Smith uses the motto, "There is a difference — come and see."

12. Have a follow-up letter ready to mail to all who come for the first Sunday.

13. Establish a visitation program. The question is often asked, What type of visitation program builds a church? Some maintain that soul-winning is the basis of building a church, and a young man should go out to lead people to Christ. Others feel that a new church needs exposure. Therefore,

enlist as many helpers to contact as many people as possible, inviting them to the new church. Some great soul-winning churches have been established by both methods, so neither excludes the other. By soul-winning visitation, new babes are brought into the church. This is the purpose of the church. But house-to-house visitation will find mature Christians who may be languishing in dead churches. Older Christians can give money, teach classes and win souls. Rudy Holland balances these contrasting opinions: "The visitation program will net those people who have been made aware of your church as a result of advertising. Your church should have an active visitation program, teaching soul-winning as a vital part of visitation. Emphasize every visit primarily as a soul-winning call and only secondarily as a church prospect call."

III. THE RIGHT ORGANIZATION

When new life is brought into the world, there is excitement. The church is an organism; it lives. But the church is also an organization. If clothing is inadequate for a human body, it may suffer or die. Some new churches have been born in hope, only to die because of inadequate "clothing." They have the correct message but have neglected proper *organization*. The following points will help the new pastor organize his church for efficient outreach and effective teaching:

1. Make sure you build a pastor-led church (Acts 20:28).

2. After the church is about one month old, plan for the organizational service. The pastor should be voted in officially and the church's name and pastor's salary established. Elect the church clerk and treasurer.

3. Wait at least one year before electing deacons. Time is needed to fully know people and allow leadership to arise.

4. Train personal soul-sinners. Set up a schedule and train people at a definite time each week. Actually take them on soul-winning tours. Continually enlist new people to train. A pastor should keep multiplying himself by training others to help him evangelize.

5. Use the Bible in your Sunday School and preaching. This will make your ministry different from most churches. People want to hear what the Bible says.

6. Have warm informal services. Make sure the singing communicates the gospel to people's hearts. People are sick of highly formal worship services. Rudy Holland observes, "It is wise to be careful of the type music used. Remember, starting with "sangin" will make it difficult to improve the music later. I recommend that good solid music be chosen. In the early days of a church, there may be little music used. It is better to have no music at all in a new church than to have music which does not glorify Christ."

7. Plan each worship service in an organized manner. Holland explains, "I do not mean formalism. Many independent Baptists pride themselves on being unorganized. This can be a real detriment to a new church. People will follow only if they are assured that the leader knows where he is going. A poorly organized service usually indicates a poorly organized church."

8. Have biblical standards for workers in the church. Some young church-planters think they can use anyone in a new church with the view of "preaching hard" in the future and raising the standards. The early life of the church is predictive of its continuing ministry. It is almost impossible to overcome weaknesses built into a new church.

9. Open a bank account for the church immediately. Many times, the church-planter will have to sign the checks until a treasurer is elected at the organizational service. The bank account should be in the name of the church.

10. Call legal aid and ask for a lawyer's help in organizing the church. It costs approximately $150 to be incorporated, plus the lawyer's fees. If the legal aid cannot help, perhaps a lawyer from a like-faith church will incorporate the church and reduce his fee. Carl Godwin waited a month after the first service to contact a lawyer. Some have incorporated before the first service.

11. Start with three classes in Sunday School: (a) Adult (youth and older); (b) Primary; (c) Nursery (Godwin made a big deal out of the nursery, even in his first flyer. To do this, some furniture and cookies are needed); and (d) Add the Junior class later.

12. Buy hymnals and offering plates.

13. Have visitors' cards ready.

14. Get offering envelopes.

15. Prepare the church constitution. Most young churches will not have knowledgable Christians who can prepare this document.

The church-planter will usually know more about the business affairs of the church than any other in the congregation. Therefore, he should prepare the constitution and bylaws (See Appendix.) The document should be printed and distributed to all members. They should be given opportunity to discuss it at a prayer meeting or in the Adult Sunday School Class. The congregation will vote its approval, but since they are a young group, the pastor should give leadership in getting this time-consuming job done.

16. Gather a qualified staff. In a small church the music, youth and Sunday School will be guided by laymen since the church lacks finances for full-time assistance. However, Perry Purtle reported, "I determined to build a staff before I built a building. People will come because of our well-rounded program, not because of our building. The best money I can spend is on a staff member. I will borrow money to hire a staff, if necessary. I called a full-time co-worker the first week. We are one year old but I have five on the staff; three are full time and two part time." Not everyone agrees with Dr. Purtle, but no one can argue his success. He called his long-time friend, J. E. Hughes, and the two made a pact to share equally the finances that came in.

17. The financial stability of a church will determine to a degree its growth. Money is needed to operate a growing church. The Bible teaches that the church should be supported by the tithes and offerings of God's people. Many pastors cannot do the things they feel God would have them do because of a financial deficiency. Rudy Holland testifies, "I have found that people give only if they are made to feel obligated to do so. Thus, it behooves every young pastor to know how to take an offering. I would recommend a simple four-step procedure in taking an offering. This is not original with me. An evangelist once told me these steps and I have found them successful."

a. Point out the financial need. You may mention the need for buses, buildings, general operating expenses, or any number of things, but let the people know the financial need.

b. Encourage every person to have a part in the offering. There are very few people who cannot give; therefore, ask everyone to have a part in the offering, even the children. A small child can have the satisfaction of helping build a new church. This will not only increase the offering, but will make everyone feel he can participate in this part of the service. Never fear asking for money. Remember, people are being asked to avail themselves of the blessings of God (Mal. 3:10).

c. Give every person an offering envelope. This encourages people to give because it provides a confidential means of giving. Many people would be embarrassed to let others see what they drop in the plate. Also, explain to people they should have a record of their giving so they can evaluate the extent of their giving. Are they giving what they should? Since God keeps records, so should your people. Then they have records for income tax.

d. Tell every person to ask God what he would have him give. As pastor, point out that God knows the financial need; he knows what part each of your people should have in the offering. If all are obedient to God, they will be blessed and the need will be met.

Holland added, "I certainly do not mean you should go through all these steps every time you take an offering, but some of these points will be profitable each time an offering is received."

One major problem with a new church is financing the building. The Berean Baptist Church in Roanoke financed its four buildings by issuing church bonds. This is a good method for financing a new church, inasmuch as most banks will not loan to new congregations. Usually, the most important factor in the issuance of church bonds is working with a qualified, reputable bond company. Some churches end up in trouble with bond programs because they deal with bond companies that are only interested in making profit. If conventional financing can be secured, it should be used. But if not, any church can have a successful bond program if operated in the right manner.

In reference to bond programs, the pastor should acquaint himself with the state laws regarding church bonds. Obtain a good general knowledge of the strengths and weaknesses of church bonds before trying to sell your people on the program. The bond program success rests largely upon the pastor. Never make the purchase of a church bond sound like a charitable donation. The public is lending you its money.

The size of the bond issue will differ in each church according to income, mortgage value, growth pattern, and operating expenses.

A good rule of thumb, especially for an established church, is that the payments for land and building should never exceed one-third of the income. Berean Baptist Church has held payments for buildings down to one-fourth of the weekly income.

CONCLUSION

The suggestions in this chapter are just that—suggestions. A church-planter may use all or none of them. These were gleaned from the ten churches in this book, plus other pastors interviewed. The men of these churches would not agree with every point, but their patterns of church planting are similar enough so that there is a general blueprint to guide those who would follow the example of Christ who said, "I will build my church" (Matt. 16:18).

CHAPTER THIRTEEN

CHOOSING A LOCATION

Finding the correct location for a church is crucial. Some young preachers indicate, "I just let God lead me to the spot." Such a reply sounds pious, but some preachers have been "led" to the wrong spot. Other ministers have begun churches only to realize years later that God providentially led to an ideal location. Dallas Billington built his first building on the property next to Reimer Elementary School, Akron, Ohio, where he began the church. Billington never conceived of filling the marsh area at the back of the property for one of the largest church parking lots which was necessary to build America's largest Sunday School. When Billington began his church in 1934, few in his congregation had automobiles; yet, God had prepared a place.

On the other hand, some churches strangle their growth because they have the wrong location. Years ago, Methodist Bishop Francis Asbury was critical of the poor location of many Methodist churches.[2] He stated:

"Some benevolent man would give us a site, the ground being so poor you could not raise mullein stalks on it. We would thank him and erect a house on it where the people would be sure not to find it. I tell you what it is; if we wish to catch fish, we must go where they are, or where they are likely to come. We had better pay money for a site in a central position

[2] Paul N. Garber, *The Methodist Meeting House*. New York: The Methodist Church, 155th Ave., 1941, p. 39.

137

in a city, town or village, than have them give us half a dozen lots for nothing in some by-street or lane."

This chapter deals with three aspects of finding a church location. First, how a pastor-planter chooses a neighborhood. Second, what should be used for the first church home. Third, how to find the best location after the church-planter has found the city or neighborhood.

I. THE RIGHT CITY

Finding the right city is important. Many of the men in this book talked with older pastors regarding a location. Jerry Falwell suggested Richmond, Virginia to Danny Smith. Carl Godwin went back to his boyhood hometown in Lincoln, Nebraska. Jim Mastin went to several cities around Chicago, trying to find a city that was needy. When Rudy Holland saw the lights of Roanoke, Virginia late one night as he drove home from college, he knew that was his Jerusalem.

God will lead the pastor-planter to the correct neighborhood, but this process is not effected by feelings. God leads through facts and, as a pastor-planter studies all the aspects of a community, God lays a city upon his heart. This is the leadership of God. A man knows he is being led of the Spirit when he has: (1) a spiritual burden for the city, (2) an inner desire to build a church there, and (3) a lack of alternative locations. Jerry Falwell told Danny Smith, "If you can go anywhere else, God is not leading you to Richmond."

Being led of the Spirit is more than an internal leading. God guides through circumstances. Perry Purtle followed the principle of need: "I began looking for a place that was not populated with strong, fundamental churches. To assist me in this search, I contacted a reputable realtor (very important). Even though I did not do it this time, if I had it to do over again, I would also hire a lawyer. I would ask him to check into the land I had selected to make sure there were no city ordinances against building a church."

Need seems to be the greatest force in guiding a man to a city. If there is no gospel-preaching church in an area, the city needs a man who will begin a gospel-preaching church. However, need alone is not enough to draw a man to a city. Every area is needy no matter how many churches are in the town. I know of no town in America that is over-saturated with the gospel. Every area has a multitude of unsaved, unchurched individuals. However, if there are New Testament churches in the area, there is a greater likelihood that the lost have at least have heard the gospel. Therefore, a young man is counseled to go start a church in one of the unchurched areas.

Dr. Max Helton of Hyles-Anderson College has a map in his office with 100 pins locating the most needy cities in America (1973-74). As a young man goes to an area and begins a church, Helton replaces the pin with a different color to indicate that a pioneer work is in operation.

When Dr. David Stauffer received his Ph.D. from seminary in 1973, he wanted to start a church. He chose St. Louis because it was one of the top ten metropolitan areas in the nation, and, according to him, "the only town where there has never been a great growing fundamental church." He arrived in town, pulling all his furniture on a rental trailer. He stayed in a motel a week trying to find a place to start the Calvary Christian Temple. He did an urbanology chart projecting future density, traffic patterns, population growth, trying to find a neighborhood that would span from upper-class to lower-class people. He ultimately bought seven and one-half acres in the center of four expressways in South St. Louis County. The church was started in a Manchester (Missouri) elementary school. Within a year, he was averaging over 300 in Sunday School and had 13 buses running ten routes, bringing in an average of 200 riders.

Barry Westbrook began the Gospel Baptist Temple in Claxton, Georgia because he had held a number of successful revival meetings in the area and knew God would bless his soul-winning efforts there. Of course, there were other factors, but his success in the area cannot be overlooked.

The church-planter should obtain the best city map available and mark all churches on the map, not forgetting those which are operating in homes, rented buildings, or have projected building plans. Rev. Everett L. Perry of the United Presbyterian Church suggests that churches of the same denomination should never be located closer than one and three-fourths miles from each other.[8]

[8] Everett L. Perry, "Supplement to a Guide for the Development of a New Church." Board of National Missions of United Presbyterian Church of USA, Feb. 1, 1959, p. 4.

In larger cities statistical information can be gathered from a U.S. Census Report, the city librarian, the city engineer's office, or the local building inspector. The number of births in the area can be found by checking with the Public Health Department. The U.S. Census will reveal the age-group distribution. The principals of schools can give the percentage of children who are Protestant, Jewish or Catholic. If the area is not completely built up, local builders can help estimate how many houses will be eventually built in the area and what demand will be made for new houses. This information can also be obtained from city planners, building permit office, and realtors.

After you have determined the number of houses or dwelling units in the area, determine the average number of people in the area using the formula of 3.6 persons in each dwelling unit.

Some denominations maintain that a religious survey should be taken to determine church membership before a new church is considered for an area. However, the men in this book choose an area because of need. They feel that church membership has no bearing on a man's relationship to God. Since liberal churches do not preach salvation, they go to a city under the leadership of the Holy Spirit and begin knocking on doors, winning people to Jesus Christ.

Shippey believes that 2,000 to 3,000 persons of gross population per church is a safe rate for beginning the church.[4] Carl Henry, Secretary of Survey and Research of the Board of American Missions, United Lutheran Church, states that he likes to consider 1,500 individuals to support a Protestant church in a metropolitan area.[5]

Shippey feels a new church should not be started with less than 100 families.[6] Many other denominations maintain that same ratio. However, fundamentalists have started with only one family. Some men have begun holding services with only their wives present. The eye of faith is sometimes greater than the mind of reason.

[4] Frederick A. Shippey, *Church Work in the City* (New York: Abingdon, Cokesbury Press, 1952) pp. 228-230 and

[5] A letter from Carl S. Henry as quoted in the thesis, "Beginning Churches in New Suburgan Communities," Asbury Theological Seminary, Aug. 1963, by Rodney Jones. P. 35.

[6] Shippey, *op. cit.* p. 230.

Men have gone into a community to start a church under the leadership of God, knowing He would bless and people would come to the new endeavor.

The Jews in biblical times began a synagogue when 12 heads of families could reach an agreement to start a new congregation. This is a more realistic consideration for evangelistic churches today.

Not every neighborhood is conducive to starting a church. It is more difficult to start a church in an old established neighborhood than in a new suburban development. Whereas settled residents tend to have their membership in an old church, mobile families in new neighborhoods are prospects for church membership. Therefore, a growing neighborhood or a transient neighborhood provides a better opportunity for succeeding than an old neighborhood. Those who are mobile are eager to: (1) find new friends, (2) establish new patterns of life, and (3) adapt to a neighborhood. Mobile families suffer some culture shock. (Because of a disorientation to life around them, they search for stability. A church meets their existential need.) When a person goes through geographical mobility, he also undergoes psychological mobility; hence, he is a candidate for the gospel. Having been cut off from the stability of the past, he has greater needs. He could be won to Jesus Christ.

Some might criticize the principle of building a church in a neighborhood that is most conducive to the gospel. Yet, Jesus commanded his disciples to go into a new city and if they were not received, shake the dust off their sandals (Matt. 10:14). Hence, Jesus was advocating that his disciples should endeavor to win those who are most receptive to the gospel and not invest as much time on those who would not receive the gospel. (He did not advocate avoiding those who were not receptive.) If a church-planter was seeking a location, he might spend more energies in a Protestant suburb rather than a Jewish neighborhood, knowing that he could win more to the Lord in one than the other. This does not mean he should never present the gospel to the Jews. The Bible teaches that Christ died for all and that "all have sinned and come short of the glory of God" (John 3:16; Rom. 3:23). Therefore, he should attempt to win all. But the greatest investment of his energies should be given those receptive to the gospel.

Many times those beginning independent churches become "star-struck" wanting to minister to the upper class or elite. However, money is often an insulation against the needs of life. It is hard for a rich man to enter the kingdom (Matt. 19:23,24); *hard* to get them saved, not impossible. At the same time, the poor are faced daily with the ultimate necessities of life; hence, they have a greater dependence on God's work in their life. Many times the poor will turn to Christ where the rich have a social snobbery and intellectual independence. A new church should minister among those most responsive to the gospel. Yet, it should not exclude the rich, nor aim only at the poor.

II. THE FIRST CHURCH HOME

After finding the city, the next task is finding a building for services. Most new churches must rent facilities. For this purpose, most pastors first look for public school facilities. Perry Purtle gives the following guidelines: "After determining in what area of the city I wanted to build, I then looked for a Sunday meeting place as near as possible to the area where I wanted to build. I went to the public school and rented the auditorium, where we met for a year."

Others have used any facility available: YMCA, lodge hall, firehouse, restaurant, civic auditorium, house, carport, factory, recreation center, or funeral home. This temporary building should have an auditorium large enough for growth, with some rooms for Sunday School space. Try to locate one with a piano. Get a definite commitment on the building as to when you can begin services and what the rent will be. Find out what storage space you can use at the building for hymnbooks, pulpit and supplies.

III. THE PERMANENT LOCATION

The permanent location of the church is highly important. Many young pastors have failed to realize the value of a good location. With the pressure of limited funds, they have settled for less expensive, out-of-the-way locations. The church-planter should drive through the neighborhood and take note of: (1) the public schools, (2) the shopping centers, (3) the existing churches, (4) the price and value of homes, (5) the projection of new homes, (6) the size of building lots, (7) the topography, (8) water, sewerage and gas connections, (9) industrial and other barriers on the neighborhood, and (10) the main arteries and thoroughfares.

The church-planter should get the zoning ordinances in a city to determine restrictions on his proposed church. Some require a large paved parking lot with a low ratio of parking spaces to auditorium size; and others have no such restrictions. In a day of mobility, if zoning restrictions are severe, the pastor should look to the next municipality that is more conducive to building a church.

There are four general criteria for selecting a good church site in a new community. They are: (1) accessability, (2) visibility, (3) relationship to the neighborhood, and (4) adequacy.[7]

Accessability. Accessability means members have quick and easy access to the church site. Most of the members will travel by car except for those who come by the church bus. Very few will walk to service. In our day of mobility, people will go as far to church as they drive to work. Some drive 20 miles one way to earn their paycheck. Hence, it is possible for a man to drive long distances to church. Studies have found that a man will drive 20 miles to church if it is located on the expressway. However, the same man would not drive five miles across the city in stop-and-go traffic, thinking that distance is too far. In Los Angeles, people tend to judge distances by time rather than miles. Five minutes on the expressway is not as prohibitive as 15 minutes through traffic, even though it is half the distance.

Accessability also means locating where the largest number of people are living. The people must have access to the church, but the church must also have access to the people. Sometimes, the young church will have to buy property on the edge of the city before private homes are built. Hence, their members will have to drive out to the church. However, the church will be located in the middle of housing projects within five to ten years.

Whereas, ten years ago experts were counseling against locating on heavily traveled highways because of the danger to children, most church-planters now maintain that a major artery is an excellent site. The danger to those who walk to Sunday School has disappeared. Of course, this principle applies to the United States,

---

[7] Perry, *op. cit.* p. 13-15.

not other countries where a vast majority of the population walks to church.

Visibility. The church should be visible to the neighborhood it desires to serve. If at all possible, place the building on a slight elevation so it can be seen from the street with the most traffic. Many churches have used signs to attract attention, but studies show that the public remembers the building better than any other form of media.

Before purchasing the site, check the zoning to make sure that no tall buildings or industry can be located next to the church. Not only would they hide the church from view, its image would be destroyed in the community. For some reason, Americans have a subconscious expectation that a church should be located in a residential neighborhood, not an industrial area.

One has even testified that a conspicuous site is worth more to a local church than a full-page advertisement in the newspaper every day of the year. This claim is probably exaggerated, but does support the argument for a good location.

Relationship to the neighborhood plan. The church should be located near the focal point of the neighborhood. Hence, residents pass it each day on their way to shop or work. If it is possible, locate the building near a shopping center so that the parking lot serves a dual purpose. Unfortunately, property near a shopping center is usually too expensive for a church.

A location near an elementary or high school is sometimes a focal point in the community. Here, a church has accessability and visibility. Also, it is near people, its point of ministry.

Adequacy. The church site must be adequate to complete its entire program. Whereas, a few years ago churches were buying four or five acres, now young men are looking for ten acres or more. Some have even purchased a church campus of 100 acres. A building site may be attractive, but when considering a complete program, it may be far too small. If a pastor-planter has a great vision, he will need a larger amount of space to carry out his ministry. Space is needed for parking, driveways, buildings, walkways, and expansion. Rudy Holland maintains, "Never consider less than ten acres for a new church site. I suggest seeking land on a major highway or city thoroughfare. God's work deserves the best location in town." Berean Baptist Church is on

11.482 acres of land, centered ⅞ mile from Interstate 81 on Exit 41. This is four blocks north of Highway 460, on City Bypass 419. Holland believes his location is an important factor in his church growth.

Check the master plan of the city to see if a future freeway or highway expansion will divide or partition part of your ground. Also, check other regulations such as setback requirements, flood planes, and amount of parking that will be allowed in the future. Some cities have not allowed churches to build on large acreages because the property would be tax free. Some city fathers feeling that they need tax income will not zone a large acreage for a church campus.

If the site does not already have water, sewerage, and gas connections, the expense should be added in the total site cost. If a well must be driven or sewer lines constructed, the cost may be excessive. In some areas a church may have to install septic tanks; for commercial use they must be large and expensive. Some churches have had to build complete sewerage installation plants costing over $100,000.00.

A new pastor should find an acreage almost immediately and place a down payment on the property (unless an abandoned church building is available). The fact of owning property will give cohesiveness and permanence to a young congregation. As soon as new property is secured, place a sign, "Future Home of _____ Church." This will give the responsibility of ownership to your people and advertise your existence to the community.

CHAPTER FOURTEEN

QUESTIONS ABOUT CHURCH PLANTING

There are questions regarding beginning a new church which require more than procedural answers. These are doctrinal issues that give direction to a young man starting a church. This chapter will be structured with questions and answers to help the reader examine the issues and come to his own conclusions.

Can Anyone Begin a Church?

The question is occasionally asked, "What agent/agency does God use to constitute a local church?" Some feel that only a New Testament church can constitute another church. They feel this way because of their doctrine of baptism—every person must be baptized by a person who has been properly immersed. This view is called "Landmarkism." Its adherents believe a new group of people cannot begin administering baptism or the Lord's table until they get authority by being organized from a duly constituted New Testament church.

There are problems with this view. First, the argument becomes continuous in time, and every local church must trace the authority of its baptism back past the mother church to the grandparent church to the great-grandparent church *ad infinitum*. When a local congregation meets God's requirement, they become a church. Then they can baptize with the authority of Christ, not the authority of the mother church.

The second argument is the church in Samaria. Philip went to Samaria and preached the gospel, baptizing them (Acts 8:12-17), before the Jerusalem church sent Peter and John down to determine the Samarian church's credibility. Also, the church at Antioch was apparently organized and responsible for a great revival long before the mother church at Jerusalem put its stamp of approval on the new congregation (Acts 11:21-24). So, new churches in the Scriptures began without the vote of approval from another congregation.

Third, Jesus is the agent that founds the church. He called it "my church," meaning a congregation belongs to him. Also, he states, "I will build," indicating that a group of people must be put together by Jesus Christ to qualify for being a local church. The word for church, *Ecclesia,* means "to call out." Jesus calls men to salvation and places them in his body, the church. This is how he builds the church. Christ is the architect, designer, contractor and, finally, he occupies the church. "And hath put all things under His (Christ) feet, and gave Him to be the head over all things to the church, which is the body" (Eph. 1:22-23). Christ also fills the church with his light (John 8:12); hence, it is called a candlestick. Obviously, Christ fills the church with his fulness causing us to say the church is equivalent to Jesus Christ, from beginning to end. Just as the body belongs to the head, Christ is the head of each local body. When Christ does the work, it is the church. Therefore, the organizational meeting is just "recognition day." As I said at one service, "We're just watching what God is doing. My organizational powers won't make this church any more spiritual . . . any more powerful . . . it won't even make this congregation an authentic church. If God has built you, this congregation is now a church."

Landmarkism believes a new local church becomes authentic when it is organized by an existing New Testament church. However, Jesus Christ is the agent who makes a church authentic.

Fourth, many young men have gone out from fundamental colleges and started a successful New Testament church. These men were not commissioned by a New Testament church. They just went out to begin a church in obedience to the call of God, relying on the power of God, building on the Word of God. True, they have been ordained by a New Testament church and sponsored in college by that church. When they went to a new community, their home church considered them "their boy." However, there was no official commissioning service to set them aside for starting the new church. This does not mean the new congregation lacks any spiritual power because there was no official vote by the mother church. Gerald Fleming graduated from Baptist Bible Seminary, Fort Worth and went to Dayton, Ohio, struggling for weeks before a group of people began meeting regularly. Bruce Cummings also graduated from Baptist Bible Seminary, knowing he wanted to start a church somewhere in Ohio or West Virginia. God led him to Massillon, Ohio, and a church of 2,000 evolved; once again, without a sponsoring church.

Other New Testament churches grew out of existing congregations and at a time in their existence, became a church. Curtis Hutson was a part-time postman and pastor in Decatur, Georgia when he read in a discarded issue of *The Sword of the Lord* that Dr. Jack Hyles baptized over 2,000 converts in one year. Thinking the statistic was a mistake, Hutson went to hear Hyles speak. While listening to Hyles give his famous lecture on soul-winning, Hutson realized two things. First, he determined his was not a church. He determined to go back and preach the Word according to the commandments of Jesus Christ. Second, Hutson determined that he could win souls. The following Saturday, he led three people to Jesus Christ. There has not been a week since that time that Hutson has not led someone to Jesus Christ. The Forrest Hills Baptist Church grew and became a true New Testament church without the sponsorship of another congregation.

Fifth, some New Testament churches have started a mission congregation which failed. If there was any magical success to rub off from the mother church, insuring the existence of its children, surely the new church would have had it. But some New Testament churches have had failure in their home mission work.

Even though we maintain a mother church is not necessary to authenticate a New Testament church, this is the way God usually works. It is usually best for one local church to start another one. Nature teaches us that like begats like, and vibrant New Testament churches begin similar churches. By this means the new congregation has the correct blueprint to insure success.

Jesus Christ uses human instruments to establish new churches. The church at Samaria was begun by Philip. He preached (Acts 8:5), won souls (Acts 8:6), and they were baptized (Acts 8:12).

Since baptism has a twofold meaning: (1) personal testimony, and (2) being added to the church, Philip must have realized the church in Samaria had been brought into existence. The church at Antioch sent out Barnabus and Saul to start churches (Acts 13:1,2). One of the criteria for a New Testament church is the evidence of spiritual gifts and leadership (Eph. 3:7-12).

Many young men in the Baptist Bible Fellowship have gone out from the Baptist Bible College, Springfield, Missouri and started successful churches.[8] Their success is not that they were sponsored by a mother church (many of them were not). Rather, their success came from the spiritual motivation they received from Baptist Bible College and the church where they were saved. They were taught correct doctrine and correct methods. Because they followed God's pattern, he blessed their efforts and used them to build great New Testament churches.

Not everyone can begin a church. A man must be called into full-time service. This call involves a burden to win souls, a desire to preach and a compulsion that a man cannot do anything else in life. A man must surrender to this "call" and prepare himself accordingly. When he is ordained, it is an outward recognition that he is called by God.

Next, God leads that man to a community to begin a church. Or in some cases, a group of lay people have a burden to start a church. After they pray, God leads to them a man to establish a church. Since one of the criteria for a church is leadership, a church cannot come into existence without the guidance of God's man.

To set this question in perspective, a pastor cannot baptize unless he is properly baptized. Neither will he baptize unless the new group is a duly constituted New Testament church.

Should a Man Begin a Church in His Home Town?

Many of the young men in this church went back to their hometowns and started churches. In so doing, they have followed the example of several pastors of growing churches.

There are several advantages in returning home to begin a a church. It is an area where the church-planter: (1) knows his

---

[8] The Baptist Bible College is used as an example because since its founding in 1950, over 1,500 of its graduates have begun a church.

way around, (2) has many friends, (3) already has a natural love and burden, (4) understands the community background and culture, and (5) would naturally remain a long time, giving opportunity to build a stable work without being called to another location. I find a great number of men in America returning to the boyhood home to either become pastor of an established church or to begin a new one. Perhaps these men are reacting to the American mobility—we are a rootless society in a floating world. They have a natural desire to settle down and build a stable church. When a young man looks around for a permanent neighborhood, the most natural place is back home.

However, one obstacle a young man faces in returning home is found in the exhortation, "A prophet hath no honor in his own country," (John 4:44). Some quote this verse to prove a preacher should leave his home town and go minister elsewhere. This appears to be a natural explanation. However, a close inspection of the verse and context reveals otherwise. First, Jesus returned and ministered to his own area even though they did not believe him. Second, the verse says nothing about successful ministry in his home town; it indicates only that he is "without honor." A pastor does not need honor in the community to be successful. He will be honored by his church. He must have the power of God upon his life and follow the guidelines of the New Testament. Third, other biblical spokesmen went back to their own people, such as Paul who was ministering in Tarsus when Barnabas called him (Acts 11:25). The Old Testament prophets preached to their own people, as did Jesus' disciples (Mark 2:21-31, 2:1-12).

After writing the book, *The Ten Largest Sunday Schools,* I noted that those who built the largest churches settled down in one location for a lifetime ministry. For the past few years, I have urged young men to settle down and invest their life in one community, building a strong New Testament church. Out of this urging some young men have returned home to build a church. This raises the question, "How does God lay a city upon a young man's heart?" and "How does God lead a minister to a city?" Sometimes the natural love a man has for a city can be used of God to become a supernatural call.

How Can an Established Church Help a New Church Get Started?

At times, the more help that is given to a new church, the less it seems to grow. Like children, it is possible to do too much for them and spoil them. The Grant Memorial Baptist Church of Winnipeg, Canada had five mission works in outlying communities during the '60's. None of these works became a church even though the mother church did much for them.

On the other hand, some mission churches die because they don't get needed help. Bill Monroe had started Florence Baptist Temple, South Carolina and was selling products door to door to make a living. The church was struggling financially as was Monroe. The Bible Baptist Church of Savannah, Georgia began sending $100 a week. "I worked more enthusiastically than ever," testified the energetic pastor. The church thrived. Four years later, they have an auditorium that seats 1,200 with an average attendance in Sunday School of over 900.

The young church needs help, but what kind and how much? First, financial support can help its growth. This can be a weekly stipend or the gift of land. Maybe the very young congregation would prosper if it had the down payment on its first building, either as a gift or as a loan. But a warning is necessary. When money is given with "strings," it can hurt rather than help. A large Presbyterian church established several mission churches, but the Board of Elders at the mother church insisted on control of the finances, approval of business, and appointment of all new pastors. The people in the mission congregation did not feel the obligation of the ministry; therefore, they never supported it with their service or gifts. The missions all eventually died.

Dallas Billington began a number of churches throughout Ohio from his pastorate at the Akron Baptist Temple, the largest Sunday School in America at the time. For some of these churches, he donated hymnbooks, renting buildings for others. His main contribution was leading a revival in which the new church was born. Billington's status as a church leader, along with his ability to win souls, launched the new church with a better opportunity for success, than if the pastor had begun on his own.

An established church can supply workers to help get a new church started. These can be soul-winners, bus workers, musicians or teachers loaned on a temporary basis. At other times families can be sent permanently to help establish a new work.

An established church shouldn't consider itself too small to help a new work get started. The Rincon Baptist Temple, Rincon, Georgia sent its Wednesday prayer meeting offering to a new work in Metter, Georgia. At the Ohio monthly meeting of pastors in the Baptist Bible Fellowship, new works are encouraged. Each month, testimonies of pastors in new churches are given. Some large churches contribute directly to the new church (not going through a central treasurer). But most amazing of all is the struggling churches that give sacrificially to churches weaker than themselves.

Should a Man Attempt to Start a Church Through a Home Bible Study Group?

None of the churches in this book grew out of a home Bible study, although some churches have come from home Bible study groups, growing into New Testament churches. The home Bible study group is a new phenomenon in our nation. Some of these are called "cell-groups," or "the living room church," or "the underground church." [9] Basically, they are people meeting togetther to study the Word of God with an attempt to apply its principle in their lives. The home Bible study is an evangelistic technique that takes advantage of American desire for dialogue and sharing. In a society of anonymity, people desire to share their problems and insight regarding the Word of God. Some are brought to a knowledge of Jesus Christ; others strengthened in their Christian life.

The churches in this book were clearly conceived in the mind of the pastor who went to a community with a view of "calling out" individuals to establish a New Testament church. None of them slowly evolved into a church.

When Royal Blue (a man's name) went to Redding, California in 1962, he found a group of Christians who were meeting for prayer and Bible study—a group honestly seeking to do God's will. He recognized immediately that here was a group of people who had faith in God and trusted God to do exceeding abundantly above all that we could ask or think. The group called themselves the Community Bible Fellowship and were not a group of community disgruntles. Sherman Fulkerth, who was then Mayor of Redding, California was the man giving direction to this small

---

[9] These groups are not New Testament churches even though they are given the title "church." However, when they grow and meet the criterion of the New Testament church, they become one.

group. Royal Blue had worked with the large First Baptist Church of Van Nuys, California as Youth Pastor.

Blue told the people when he came to Redding, "You haven't told the city anything by using the name Community Bible Fellowship." Blue also indicated that the Bible Fellowship had not established doctrine; therefore, there was no basis on which members could join the group, nor were the people obligated to the group. He said the name "Community Bible Fellowship" could be a conglomeration of a number of beliefs, and even people from cults could be involved. "I am a Baptist, and I believe in establishing churches," he told the people in the initial meeting. He commented that several from the Navigators had been involved in the prayer group, and he endorsed people getting into the Word, finding salvation and stabilizing their lives. However, Blue noted, "We must do more than get *into* the Word, we must get *under* the Word, and let the Bible give direction both to us as individuals and to us as a group." He also encouraged the people to obey the Lord's command to baptize new converts by immersion and to celebrate the Lord's Supper.

Blue did not set a goal to build a large church, but testified, "I conceived of a group of people who wanted to witness and take the gospel to the entire city of Redding and to the regions of Northern California." Out of North Valley Baptist Church has come the direction that is being afforded to 16 smaller churches in the Northern California area, all growing and reaching souls for Christ.

Some of those who preach in these churches are lay leaders from North Valley Baptist, and some have become full-time pastors. Jack Jones, one time Chairman of the Board of Deacons at North Valley Baptist, has become Pastor of the Palo Cedro Community Baptist Church, working full time. He also has three staff members full time.

Today, the North Valley Baptist Church has over 1,800 members, a Sunday morning attendance of over 1,300 worshippers, and a weekly offering of between $6,000 and $7,000. This year their missionary budget calls for $50,000. The church property is valued at over one million dollars, and it has a youth camp at one-half million dollars. God is using the members of this church to influence others of the Northern California area; something that just a Bible study group could never have accomplished.

Most Bible study groups lack three qualities that have excluded them from being included in this book. A Bible study is not a church but is a technique that can be used by a church. The Kansas City Baptist Temple has reached many young married couples for Christ, bringing them into this strong evangelistic church. Roscoe Brewer, Sunday School Coordinator, gathers young couples together during the week to involve them in the Word of God. But, he makes sure they are involved in the church. A Bible study group can become a New Testament church. This happens when all the characteristics of a local church become evident.

1. *A Bible study group usually lacks a leader committed to founding a church.* The genius of a Bible study group is interaction, each man sharing his insight from the Bible. Discussion, not a sermon, is the catalyst that makes it successful. Sometimes, those in a Bible study group come from many churches; other times, group members come from an unchurched background.

2. *A Bible study group lacks commitment to church ordinances.* The ordinances of Baptism and the Lord's Table belong to the local church. Individuals should not practice these ordinances, nor should a Bible study group until they are constituted as a New Testament church. Even though a pastor gathers people to study the Bible, they should not practice the ordinances apart from a New Testament church. When a group of Christians organize themselves according to the New Testament, they will want to obey the two commands: (1) "Go and make disciples . . . baptizing them" (Matt. 28:19), and (2) "Take eat, this is my body" (I Cor. 11:23,24). Since these are commands of our Lord, the Christian who does not join himself to a church that observes the ordinances properly cannot be in the perfect will of God.

3. *A Bible study group does not have an obligation to corporate ecclesia (the embryonic church) through mutual fellowship, attendance, financial support, and numerical growth.* Many attend a Bible study group because of the personal enrichment they receive. (This is an honest contribution to the cause of Christ.) However, the same Christians would have grown more spiritually if they had been members of a church where they accepted the obligations that would have developed them greater. When an individual accepts the obligation of membership in a New Testament church, he

must financially support the group, understand its doctrine, support its services, and involve himself in Christian service through that church. An individual becomes a better Christian by placing himself under the discipline of a church.

How Important Are Buildings and Property to a New Church?

The acquisition of buildings and property is more important in American church growth than at other times in past history. In the early church, Christians met on Solomon's porch for preaching and fellowship. Also, they met in private homes, in the school of Tyrannus, in open amphitheaters and caves. There has always been some central focal place for assembly. Since the first century of Christianity, Christians have constructed buildings. In our century, God has used many unusual locations to establish local churches. A boat house in Garland, Texas launched the LaVonne Drive Baptist Church. The Central Baptist Church in Phoenix, Arizona first met around picnic tables in a park. Trinity Baptist Church in Chattanooga, Tennessee was begun in a carport, and Calvary Baptist Church in Ft. Lauderdale, Florida was begun in a display home. In addition to these, churches have been begun in feed stores, fire departments, abandoned grocery stores, lodge halls, funeral homes, bankrupt soft drink bottling plants and other buildings that brought a young congregation out of the elements. As temporary as these permanent buildings were, an element of stability was added when a congregation moved into its own building.

Some advocate that a church should remain in rented facilities, not investing its money in buildings. One pastor desired to remain in a rented public school; the congregation was too poor to buy property and construct a building. To this day, they are still too poor and remain in the rented school. They argue that too much money can be involved in mortar, glass and steel—money which could be used for missions. As valid as this argument is, the church will have more to give to missions by following prescribed methods of growth.

The pastors in this book realize what moving into their own building can do to strengthen a young church. Rudy Holland in Roanoke, Virginia indicated many families remained on the fringe, watching the young church as it met in the rented facilities of the civic center. But when it moved into its own facilities, the attitude of Christians on the outside changed. Families began joining. These families brought financial strength, teaching abilities and maturity with them. Holland explains, "Don't criticize these people for lack of pioneering zeal. They had an honest doubt. When we bought property and built, they knew we were not a flash in the pan."

When a congregation moves into its own facilities, it gains the following advantage: (1) the community realizes the church is permanent, no longer a transient group; (2) the young congregation becomes a part of the city, a property holder; (3) the young congregation identifies with the neighborhood, they belong to the landscape and the community; (4) permanent facilities allow people to funnel their energies into other ministry rather than preparing the building each week. Danny Smith indicates each week he had to set up chairs, distribute hymnbooks, and get the building ready for a meeting. Jim Mastin at Milwaukee indicated each Saturday night he labored until 2 or 3 A.M., getting the building ready for Sunday services. Many times they had to sweep up the cigarette butts and take out the beer cans before holding church in the YMCA. He complained, "Our teachers couldn't hang a picture and didn't use as many visual aids because they had to drag flannel boards in and take down pictures after each class."

When interviewing the pastors of the ten largest Sunday Schools, most reiterated, "Never get out of a building campaign." By this, they meant a church should always plan another building for added growth. Christianity is a process, not a product. Therefore, the young congregation should always be building additional rooms or enlarging the auditorium. Physical expansion reflects spiritual growth and, if a church is winning souls, they will need more space to teach and preach. Also, when the neighborhood sees additions being built, they realize the church is growing.

Even though the building only houses the meetings of the church, Americans still judge a church by its buildings. Sloppily kept buildings indicate a messy attitude toward Christianity. When a congregation will sacrifice to build an auditorium, they tell the community that preaching is important.

Because I feel a building and property are important, I have insisted on the establishment of a building fund in many of the young churches I have organized. Then, I personally contributed to this building fund, knowing that dollars in the bank is a tangible incentive to a young congregation. Carl Godwin began looking for 20 acres of ground when the church was less than 20 weeks old. He knew that a tangible location would build a sense of belonging in his young congregation. Perry Purtle acquired property almost immediately, and the congregation knew it was there to stay!

Should the Church-Planter Spend His Time Winning New Converts or Recruiting Older Christians?

When Carl Godwin was interviewing pastors before beginning his church in Lincoln, he asked about the foundation of a new church. Some pastors told Godwin not to proselyte older Christians from other churches because they had poor church habits and were usually the malcontents. "Go door-to-door and win your whole congregation to Christ," one pastor told Godwin "Then you have a church that will be pure and zealous to serve Christ." The older pastor continued, "These new Christians will follow your leadership and you can build a church without friction."

When Godwin founded Calvary Bible Church in Lincoln, he changed his thinking. His young Christians were not trained to come to Sunday services. They didn't tithe, and some had problems with sins. These new babes in Christ were a thrill to Godwin, but they were not stable enough to help build a church. God sent the church some mature Christians from other churches who could lead souls to Christ and teach Sunday School. These were not malcontents, but were Christians who had been praying for an aggressive soul-winning church in their city.

On the other hand, while Godwin was interviewing older pastors, one directed him to get a nucleus of mature Christians to add stability to the young congregation. Some new churches are built almost exclusively on older Christians. These churches are founded by groups that have come out of another church, perhaps to preserve pure doctrine or to repudiate sin in the former assembly. These churches usually don't grow rapidly but do a commendable job of ministering the Word of God.

Sometimes, older Christians have the stability of time-proven endurance, but they lack the zeal of the young convert who is carried along by his love for Christ.

Alden Laird founded Hyland Hills Community Church in Denver (fall 1973) without older Christians. He spends much of his time working with young converts, testifying, "I don't have time to knock on doors, I'm so busy looking after the needs of young converts."

The church-planter faces the alternative of building his church on door-knocking (evangelism) or on ministering to mature Christians. The answer is in neither extreme but in a combination of the enthusiasm of young Christians and the maturity of the old. But with this combination, never forget evangelism. The purpose of a church is winning the lost to Jesus Christ. The young church, like the old churches, can lose their candlestick when they lose their soul-winning perspective of evangelism.

Is There a Certain Personality Trait in Men Who Establish Churches?

Some often ask if there is a personality type that is more successful in starting churches. Some think the church-planter must be the rugged individualist who can persevere in spite of the odds. Others think he must be a charismatic personality attracting people to himself, hence building the church on his own charm. From my observation, I have seen all types of men build churches. Bill Monroe who founded the Florence Baptist Temple was shy in meeting people, yet aggressive in doing the work of God; so was Carl Godwin in Lincoln, Nebraska. Rudy Holland is the unstoppable force who can plow through the immovable object—with love. Bud Calvert is sophisticated and would be at home with the executive; so is Perry Purtle. Each builder of churches has his own strengths and weaknesses. Other men begin churches in rural areas with dogged determination that attracts the rugged farmer.

Since Jesus is the founder of the church, he uses human channels who are dedicated to him. Only God can accentuate a man's talents, while at the same time compensating his weaknesses. God uses the inadequate individual with meager abilities and marginal equipment to serve in limited circumstances. When he is God's man, he beats insurmountable odds, overcoming oppressive obstacles to accomplish a work of God. Never was this more demonstrated than in the ten men who founded these churches.

Men who start churches must be pioneers, and only certain men have that trait. These men must be willing to swing a hammer and negotiate a loan. They must promote in the pulpit and advertise in the newspaper. They must preach, counsel, rebuke and teach the Bible. A pioneer must be able to do it all, for he usually begins with little if any help. The pioneer must lead people to Christ, nurture them in the Scriptures, train them in service and inspire them to spiritual greatness.

Some church pioneers go from one challenge to another. They have ruggedness to "plant" but lack the patience to "water" (I Cor. 3:6). Praise God for church-planters. Missionary Lonnie Smith in Monterrey, Mexico has planted over 30 churches. Praise God for pastors who build. Dallas Billington did both, founding the Akron Baptist Temple and building it to over 6,000 in Sunday School.

The man who would begin a church must be *humble,* realizing that it is God who works through all of his abilities no matter how strong or lacking. He must have vision as the prophet of the Old Testament called a *seer,* (I Sam. 9:9) because he was the eyes for God—seeing first, seeing farthest, and seeing the most. The man who would start a church must by faith see the church completed in his heart before a soul is won or a brick is laid on the foundation. *Courage* is another attribute of the church-planter, he must face discouragement and disappointment. Some of those he leads to Christ will turn their backs on the Lord. Other young babes in Christ will not grow according to his expectations. No congregation will grow as rapidly as the pastor expects, nor will the new building be as elaborate as the pastor desires. He needs courage to accept the present without letting discouragement rob his future. *Compassion* is another needed quality. Who can build a church without the love of God flowing through him? The church-planter must love people, want to be with them and desire to serve them. *Tenacity* is needed in every successful life. The church-planter cannot build a church without persevering; he must never give up. A new church is an endless struggle. Because he senses God's call to a community, he does not turn back because of opposition. Because he has a burden from God for a city, he rejects calls to settled pastorates and established salaries. "Jesus steadfastly set his face to go to Jerusalem," (Luke 9:51) where he would die for his people. The church-planter must have the same determination. He will build a church because he made a promise to God and to himself.

The church-planter must embody all the qualities of the Christian life because, as the shepherd of the flock, he is their example. Being controlled by the Spirit in his preaching, teaching, soul-winning and church management is only the first step. The church-planter must display the fruit of the Spirit in his personal life so that others desire to be like him. If the list of qualities for a church-planter were complete, it would be as long as the requirements for any pastor. To make the qualifications short and understandable, he must simply be "God's man" in the community, doing what Christ would do.

Can a Church be Revived When it Loses its Candlestick?

Can a church lose its candlestick (stop fulfilling the functions of a church and die, Rev. 2:5), repent, and again meet New Testament qualifications, thus becoming a church again? This is a difficult question. However, all things are possible with God. When the question was asked, "Can these bones live?" (Jer. 37:3), the answer was "Yes, in God's time." Apparently, the North Baptist Church in Brockton, Massachusetts, was once a great evangelistic church. However, over the years the church deteriorated in finances, income, and enthusiasm. In the early '70's, Gerald Kroll was called as pastor after graduating from Gordon Divinity School, Massachusetts. Gerald Kroll admitted he was an evangelical, yet searching for a better way. He read *The Ten Largest Sunday Schools,* then visited the churches in that book located in Hammond, Indiana; Detroit, Michigan; Akron and Canton, Ohio. After seeing these great soul-winning churches in action, Kroll visited the pastor's conference at Thomas Road Baptist Church, Lynchburg, Virginia. There, he determined to revive his church and began an aggressive soul-winning program. He added buses, preached for repentance, gave an invitation, organized soul-winning visitation and built a new building. Attendance jumped from 70 to over 300 in two years. When I asked Kroll if the candlestick was restored to the church during his ministry at Brockton, he replied, "I think so." Supporting his argument, he stated that for four years prior to his coming, there were no baptisms in the church.

There is a warning to laymen. Usually the only person who can "turn around" a church is the pastor. He sets the stage for spiritual growth or the lack of it. Some laymen remain in a dead church hoping to revive it. It is almost impossible for a layman to restore the candlestick. Many pastors have tried and failed. Most of the pastors in this book felt they would be farther ahead to begin a new work than to take an old church and spend years trying to turn it around.

CHAPTER FIFTEEN

CAN A CHURCH START FROM A SPLIT?

As my wife typed this section, she looked up from the keys and humorously suggested its title, "How To Split a Church to the Glory of God." She reflected the attitude prevalent in the Christian world—that a church should never split. Since Jesus said, "I will build my church" (Matt. 16:18), most think it is presumptuous to "split" a church that Christ built. It is difficult to analyze issues that lead to a church split, because splits are usually born of emotions rather than rationality. Good men have deep feelings concerning church splits.

Those who feel a church should never divide usually question any group splitting a New Testament church. The motives of any pastor who has successfully led a split are doubted. The idea of a church split is rejected even though there is some validity to this position. On the other hand, others will split a church over the smallest issue. Some, like spoiled children, will pick up their toys and go elsewhere to play (lead a fraction out of a church). A few pastors who receive a majority vote may try to "run out" those who voted against them. When people leave a church individually, this is known as splintering a church.

Church splits have their humorous side. When interviewing a pastor of a large northern church, I asked how many churches he had started. "Several . . . but none by design," he replied. Another pastor stated, "We've had so many splinterings that we have supplied kindling wood leading to revival fires all over the city."

Is there a proper way to split a congregation, bringing glory to God? Some say no! At the same time, fights, arguments, court cases, name calling, ugly scenes and adverse news coverage cannot help the cause of Christ. Paul and Barnabas had been a successful missionary team, planting churches. The two men had been friends since Barnabas had befriended Paul immediately after his salvation, when no one else would. These men were closer than any pastor and staff member. Yet, when approaching their second missionary journey, Barnabas wanted to take young John Mark along. Paul objected. "The contention was so sharp between them, that they departed asunder from one another" (Acts 15:39). God used Paul's temper to double the missionary endeavor, and two teams went out instead of one.

In one sense, most American churches come from a split. A new church in an old neighborhood is established from the same motivations that a split occurs; i.e., the old churches are not getting the job done. However, young churches in new neighborhoods are usually established out of evangelistic endeavor. The men in this book who established churches felt that the old churches were not getting the job done. Actually, these new congregations were begun by "carving a church out of a hard place." There were many churches in Roanoke, Virginia, but Rudy Holland established Berean Baptist Church. Richmond was saturated with churches, yet God moved the heart of Danny Smith to found the Open Door Baptist Church.

Men leave denominational churches to start churches, splintering their efforts because they feel their denomination is dying. Jim Singleton went to Tempe, Arizona, leaving the Southern Baptist Convention. Three families left the Nazarene Church to help found Calvary Baptist Church, Lincoln, Nebraska. Since they did not come as a unit, they cannot be called a church split. Yet each family was dissatisfied with local Nazarene churches. Over 200 people left the Highlawn Baptist Church in Huntington, West Virginia to begin the Fellowship Baptist Church. They came as a unit. Some of these had been in the previous church all their lives. Their time, money and prayers helped build their church, yet they left it behind. Usually when one family leaves an old dying church to join a young vibrant congregation, other families follow. Like the first trickle of rain cutting a trough down newly plowed dirt, the stream grows wider.

Most of the church splits I know arise over personality rather than doctrine. Individuals could not get along. Two good friends can disagree over an issue but love each other in the Lord. They remain friends, yet the same issue would split those who already have a basic dislike for each other.

In spite of all the unfortunate church splits, God has used many to his glory. People have been brought to salvation who would not have otherwise been reached. Communities have been evangelized, colleges built, missionaries sent out, and money raised that would never have come from a complacent, dead church. God causes even the wrath of man to praise his name (Gen. 50:20).

When Should a Split Occur?

The one basis over which churches should split is the candlestick (Rev. 1:19, 2:1,5). When a church is in danger of losing its existence, it should take measures that will return the candlestick to its original brilliance. (The candlestick is Christ, the Light of the World, dwelling in every believer as he joins in corporate assembly to evangelize the community.) Since the church is a unity, the responsibility of the church rests upon every member. It is the duty of the whole church to: (1) preserve unity, (2) maintain correct doctrine, (3) practice pure living, (4) elect leaders to carry out the church's purpose, and (5) exercise discipline. Each member is responsible to make sure the candlestick burns brightly. When it doesn't, they should take biblical steps to put the church in order. If they cannot correct the problem, should they stay and submit, or leave? When God removes his blessing from a church, it is time for the zealous believer to leave. As a result, a church split is not just a terrible appendage in the program of God; it is the final step when a church has lost its candlestick, or the church's existence is threatened. The following factors will help determine when a split is necessary:

1. *A church split is justified if the church is not baptizing new believers.* If new converts are not being baptized, the church is not winning souls. Therefore, the "candlestick" is in jeopardy and flickers low. This may be a basis for a group of people to leave a church and start another one. Some maintain Christians ought

to remain and serve the Lord in a dead church because they can win souls and influence a few people in their Sunday School classes. However, a layman can only do so much. The pastoral and board leadership will inevitably influence the church according to their objectives. If they are not winning souls now, there is little possibility they will do so in the future. If Christians leave and join a vibrant New Testament church, they will accomplish much more with the same energy in the new church than in the former dead church.

Usually, people remain in dead churches because of friends or the church buildings and equipment. The freedom of serving Christ in a biblical church has greater rewards, even when the facilities are less than adequate. A church is not the building or its facilities. There is a question whether faithful Christians can get control of the church property and assets when they are the minority. They can claim to be the true church because they are faithful to New Testament doctrine. But if they do not have the majority, it is best to leave; they have no other alternative.

2. *A church split is justified when doctrine is compromised.* The New Testament church was bound together in stability by the harmony of its doctrine. Even at the Jerusalem council, when they disagreed over doctrine, the churches were strong enough to override the schismatic nature of divided opinion. Church splitting over doctrine is seldom a black-white issue; there are shadows of gray that cloud the issue. When a group of people in a liberal church find Christ as Saviour, those controlling the church are not hospitable to fundamental doctrine. It is easy to see how disagreement over doctrine would cause these Christians to break off into a new church. However, a congregation is the body of Christ. A body usually grows cohesively as a unit. Therefore, if the whole church is growing in knowledge and faith, there should be no disagreement of doctrine. The people should grow together in understanding. The church should have harmony of doctrine. Yet, individual Christians will never find another person with whom they completely agree. Therefore, there will be disagreements within a church. Church splits are justified because of disagreements over major issues of doctrine, such as the virgin birth, the inspiration of Scripture or the nature of baptism. However, should churches split when they disagree over the nature of

man: i.e., one Christian feels man has a dichotomous nature, while the second believer feels man has a body, soul and spirit?

Pure doctrine is not the ultimate or only purpose of a church; it is the means to an end. The objective of a church is the Great Commission. But correct doctrine is the only foundation on which evangelism and the Christian life prosper. The Bible is the foundation of the church, and no local church could be built without correct adherence to doctrine. However, when a cohesive group of people are held together only by pure doctrine, they tend to major on minor variations of dead orthodoxy, leading to sterile sermons. In turn, this may lead to unjustified church splits.

A church may compromise its doctrine and conscience by continued affiliation with a dying denomination or affiliation with unscriptural organizations. A church may compromise its doctrine by allowing outside speakers who hold an unscriptural stand. Doctrinal compromise makes it impossible for a church to fulfill its obligation to the Scriptures and carry out evangelism; therefore, a group of people have a Scriptural basis to form a new church. This should be done only when it can demonstrate that the present church has broken fidelity with the New Testament.

3. *Impurity is another factor that can lead to a church split.* A local church, like individual Christians, should live holy lives apart from sin. Just as God will not hold the Christian blameless who sins, so God demands purity in the church. When a church permits obvious sin to persist in the congregation with no attempt to correct it, the blessing of God will be taken from that church. However, a split is justified only when sin keeps a church from fulfilling its basic purpose in life. The following cautions are in order: (1) Every church has some evil present for no man lives without sin. Therefore, no group of people is completely pure. (2) If a church is attempting to deal with its sin, a young hothead should not try to split the church. (3) There will usually exist sin in fringe members. This is not a basis for a church split. A split is justified when there is obvious compromise in the pastor, deacons, or workers.

Impurity that leads to a split may grow in two areas. First, a church allows public sin to remain in its leadership. This might be in its board members, teaching staff or pastor. These men may have unconscious sins which are not obvious to others. These will not necessarily hinder the testimony in the community. A congregation must work, pray and encourage one another in this cause. But when public sin destroys the church, those who want to remain pure should try to exercise church discipline. When it fails, they are free to establish a new church.

I believe a fundamental church recently lost its candlestick when the pastor, an evident preacher of the Scriptures, divorced his wife. The candlestick could have remained if the people had voted to remove its pastor, but they did not. Both people and pastor are living contrary to the New Testament. Can God bless this church with his presence? When Christians find themselves in a church that will live contrary to the New Testament, they should split and join/form another church.

Attitudes During Church Splits

The following attitudes can help bring glory to God in the middle of a split. Recently a denominational official said to me, "You fundamentalists are always splitting churches. We liberals never split a church." His remarks put me on the defensive. We fundamentalists seem like underdogs who take our toys and go home (start over again) when we can't get our way. I reminded him liberals don't give attention to biblical doctrine, pure life or winning souls. Since they didn't have an objective position to hold, they could drift with any current. Therefore, they wouldn't fight, nor do they have the strength of commitment to start over again; i.e., to split and begin a new church. The following principles will help guide those caught up in a church split.

1. *Keep issues centered on doctrine, not personalities.* Ever since I was a freshman in college, I have heard it said that a church split centers on people, not doctrine. There is no statistic to verify this conclusion, but it probably reflects most church splits. People get mad at the preacher and look for an issue to justify their leaving to start a new church. At other times, two factions within a congregation oppose each other. Often, when there is a doctrinal issue, it is obscured by personal feelings. Some issues are brought to congregational vote, just to "straighten" out other people in the church. When a church faces a split, examine the issues to determine if doctrine or personality is the key issue.

2. *The motive to start a new church should be to fulfill the Great Commission.* Often, a new church is started just to get away

from corruption or to find a new base for fellowship. The desire for separation from doctrinal corruption is commendable but is not a sufficient basis to start a church. Some have left a church that is squabbling, seeking peace in a new church. As much as church fights are deplored, harmony is not the ultimate purpose of founding a new congregation. A church is organized to carry out the Great Commission. Even if the new church has fundamental doctrine, it will not prosper as God wants it to prosper unless soul-winners will evangelize the neighborhood.

3. *A church split should follow the scriptural pattern of dealing with grievances.* First, when a man has a charge in his heart against a brother, he should face him with the issue. Second, the Scriptures indicate that the offended should take someone else with him when airing his grievance. Finally, the issue should be brought before the church. Here, the constitution and bylaws of the church should be followed and the grievances brought out into the open. No church split should be attempted before first bringing the issue to the church as a whole. Discuss it—rationally. Ask for people to examine Scripture and pray over the matter. Then, if nothing can be resolved, the parties who start a new church will have no guilt feelings. They have proceeded according to Scripture.

4. *Keep all motives pure.* When Christians disagree it is easy for jealousy, strife or spite to influence their feelings. Keep a sweet spirit. When Abraham's herdsmen had a disagreement with Lot, they reminded themselves, "We be brethren" (Gen. 13:8). When you disagree with other Christians, remember, they are born again by the same blood. If the church is apostate, you are not dealing with Christians; they are lost people. You have an obligation to live before them as before heathen.

5. *Don't win the battle and lose the war.* Some church splits have been so "hateful" that both sides destroy their reputation in their city. After the severance has been made, they are not able to win lost people to Christ because of their unchristian spirit. Therefore, judge every action by the "long look." The new church will have to live in the community. When a new church is born in friction, it usually "fights for its life." Beware of getting the reputation of being contentious and antagonistic. This is the wrong image for a church. Of course, you will "contend for the faith," and you will "resist the devil." Make sure the community knows

why you fight. A church should be militant, but at the same time it must be loving.

CONCLUSION

This chapter does not encourage church splits, but recognizes their inevitability. My prayer to the Lord is, "That they may be one" (John 17:11). However, because sin infiltrates the church, because men are drawn away into false doctrine, because Christians tend to grow cold in their love and because churches die, church splits are inevitable. My advice to those who split churches comes from a package of dynamite I once saw when an uncle was blasting stumps: "If you don't know what you are doing, do not touch. If you do—handle with care."

CHAPTER SIXTEEN

THE ROLE OF A PIONEER-PASTOR

Throughout the centuries, aggressive churches that have shaken communities for God have been founded by men. Whether it was John Wesley establishing preaching houses throughout England or Dwight Moody beginning Sunday Schools in Chicago, great works were established by God's man who came preaching repentance and regeneration. Two centuries ago, Adoniram Judson established churches in the heathen environment of Burma. In the past few years, Lonnie Smith has established over 30 Baptist churches in the Catholic influence of Monterey, Mexico. These aggressive churches did not grow out of community consensus, nor did they stem from a committee.

However, there have been numberless churches growing from the corporate effort of many, such as a neighborhood of farmers who felt the need of a church. They sacrificed to construct a building and called a "parson." These churches grew out of the neighborhood and served the religious needs of the community. This book is not written about establishing these community churches even though there remain places where the community church has validity.

A church should attempt to capture its town for Christ even as the first church "filled Jerusalem with its doctrine" (Acts 5:28). This volume describes going to an unchristian community, preaching the gospel, teaching young converts and establishing a church. Unchurched and unreached communities need an aggressive church to evangelize the lost and motivate Christians. Determined churches grow out of determined pastors.

The success of the churches in this book is directly related to the ability of the pastor. He is much more involved in the leadership of the church than the typical American pastor is involved in the leadership of his church.

Some have questioned if the pastor should have much to say about the finances of a church. Others have accused the pastors of aggressive churches of being dictators because he administers the business affairs of the church. This raises the question, what is the biblical role of pastor leadership?

1. *Elder* (presbuterors). As an elder, the pastor's main responsibility is to be an example to the flock by spiritual maturity. An elder denoted "seniority," historically he was a part of the deliberation assembly in Israel. Peter writes, "Likewise ye younger, submit yourselves to the elder" (I Peter 5:5). A careful study of the New Testament reveals the elder gave leadership to the flock because of his spiritual example. His duty to administer (rule) is seen in the exhortation, "Let the elders that rule well be counted worthy of double honor" (I Timothy 5:17). One of the qualifications to rule the house of God was to rule his own home. If a pastor can't lead his family (financially, spiritually, discipline, etc.) he can't lead the church. "For if a man know not how to rule his own house, how shall he take care of the church of God?" (I Timothy 3:5).

The Scriptures are abundantly clear that the pastor-elder has an administrative responsibility to the church. Paul called the elders of Ephesus (Acts 20:17) and challenged them, "Take heed therefore unto yourselves and to all the flock over the which the Holy Ghost hath made you overseers" (Acts 20:28). Overseeing the church began by personal testimony and exercised itself by leadership supervision. Peter reinforces the admonition, "taking the oversight thereof" (I Peter 5:2). Scriptures also speak to the believer to "Remember them which have the rule over you" (Hebrews 13:7), and "Obey them that have the rule over you" (Hebrews 13:17), and "To know them which labor among you and are over you in the Lord and admonish you; to esteem them very highly in love for their works sake" (I Thess. 5:12,13). The pastor-elder has more authority than is given to (or taken by) the average American pastor. He is to be respected, obeyed, and loved. Those who criticize their pastor and refuse to support his leadership need to examine Scripture.

To balance the picture, the pastor does not have a free hand to dictate his own policy. He is a man under authority. He is a servant of the flock. The scriptures warn the elders, "Take heed therefore unto yourselves" (Acts 20:28), and "Neither as being lords over God's heritage, but being ensamples to the flock" (I Peter 5:3). The word *elder* connotes spiritual maturity and the pastor who must demand allegiance from Christians reveals his lack of it. The pastor-elder elicits cooperating first by his example and second by the biblical office he holds. He must appeal to biblical truth, and display spiritual power. Anything less creates a question regarding his call by the Holy Spirit to pastor the flock.

2. *Bishop* (episcopes). The word means to oversee or to superintend. Paul's instruction to Titus (Titus 1:5) indicates an elder and bishop were the same office. The word *elder* implies the pastor's personal qualifications while the word *bishop* suggests his duties.

When a church-planter desires to be a pastor, he should heed the admonition "If a man desires the office of a bishop, he desireth a good work" (I Timothy 3:1). Work is the last word in the verse and work is the key to the success of any new church. But hard work alone will not build a church. A church-planter must fulfill the qualifications of a bishop, he must be: (1) blameless, (2) self-controlled, (3) abstainer from alcohol, (4) not seek finances, (5) have a love for souls, (6) be spiritual, and (7) committed to teach and live doctrine. (These qualifications are found in Titus 1:7-9.)

3. *Spiritual ministry.* Pastoral leadership must be exercised in light of other pastoral functions such as a (1) shepherd (poimen) where he feeds the flock (I Pet. 5:1,2); and (2) preacher (kerux) where he exhorts the congregation (II Tim. 4:2, I Cor. 14:3); and teacher (didaskalus) where he teaches the flock (Matt. 28:20).

Some churches relegate to the pastor only the spiritual duties of preaching, teaching and counseling. The fiscal and business matters are handled by deacons or the board. Such an approach to church administrators is not biblical nor is it practical. Not one verse of Scripture supports a deacon-run church. Their primary duty is service to the cause of Christ, not a legislative body to determine church policy. The criticism is often heard, "We don't want the pastor to be a dictator." I have seen worse dictatorial control of churches by deacons than I have ever seen by a pastor. But the scriptural plan is for neither to dictate policy to the church. The pastor is the leader. The deacons (or board of laymen) serve the cause of Christ and give support (advice) to the pastor in carrying out the ministry. The congregation is the final seat of authority to determine policy, direction and discipline. Hence, the church has a three-fold system of checks and balances: the pastor, the deacons and the congregation, each depending on the other while mutually supporting one another in the biblical task before them.

As I have viewed the role of pastors, most church-planters are like the self-made businessman. They are the rugged individualists. However, with time, I have seen them change in their role and self perception. As others with the gifts of leadership arise in the congregation, pastor-pioneers have changed. They work with deacons; they work through superintendents, and they work within the organization they have built. They build organizational structure, giving away some of the authority that was theirs without losing the influence of their leadership.

When discussing a change in pioneer-pastors, it is really growth we are describing. The man who has a long successful pastorate is a growing Christian. He must grow in status as his church grows in size and influence. His capacity, ability and compassion must grow as the problems of a larger congregation become more complex.

In the military, the role of leadership changes. The lieutenant who leads an attack up a hill becomes the general who plans strategy behind the lines. The pastor who lays concrete block with his men becomes the manager of a multi-million dollar corporation. What was once a high-structural management changes to a shared-management concept of leadership.

The field of management recognizes the need of a strong personality at the inception of a business. Called high-structural management, or downward cycle, the entrepreneur or businessman is the pioneer, personnel manager, visiting fireman and motivator all wrapped up in one man. The aims, motivations and evaluations reside in the man. The owner and the business are inseparable; he is the company. Usually, the employees work for the boss and have a direct relationship with him.

After the company has existed for a length of time and has grown large, new needs arise that demand a different kind of management. Employees lose contact with the boss, and bureaucracy settles over the organization with its accompanying apathy and sometimes atrophy. Shared-management, goal-setting and an upward cycle of change is necessary for business prosperity.

When a new business is started or a new management moves into an existing industry, he uses a low structural management (the typical American church). The new leader attempts to introduce change from the bottom. With this method, a training program communicates new knowledge which is supposed to change the attitudes of the employees, thus modifying individual behavior, ultimately changing group behavior. This is the upward cycle of leadership where management is shared with employees following the route of "indigenous leadership." The employee is given reasons, motivation, and training to improve his task in the company. As he improves, of course, production improves and profits rise. This is often called an upward cycle in management to curb deteriorating employee-employer relationships. The result is improved esprit de corps among the entire business.

The high-structured management begins at the top and forces coerced change downward through the system. The manager sets standards for the entire group which may be in regard to goals of production, codes of dress, regulations concerning behavior, etc. The theory of high-structured management is: (1) group behavior is the result of individual conformity to group standards; (2) individual behavior is slowly internalized; (3) the individual begins to assume the attitudes of the corporation and those who work around him. Finally, he takes on (4) the knowledge he needs to improve himself and ultimately the company.

When a pastor takes over a church in existence, he usually must use low-structured management or plan change to make upward improvement in the organization. This involves leadership training classes and education, the upward cycle having a leavening effect on the entire church. Sometimes, a young man comes into an old church with great zeal, yet lacking knowledge and uses a high-structured management trying to enforce group behavior on all church members. This usually results in (1) a split congregation, (2) the loss of certain members, or (3) the firing of the pastor.

The young man who begins the church must begin with a high-structured leadership because there is no existing organization. There must be a downward cycle because he usually personifies the standards of behavior and service in the church. The new church does not have group behavior, so it must be set by the pioneer-pastor. Dr. David Stuffer of Calvary Christian Temple, St. Louis, Missouri justified, "I had a new church with unstructured Christians. I could not let them determine the standards of the church, so I had to crack the whip with love." Stuffer, who understands business management, indicates, "I enforced a coercive style of management realizing I was causing a volatile reaction among some people, but there was no other way to get the church started." Some came and left the young church. Stuffer ultimately wants to reverse the cycle of planned change from a downward cycle to an upward cycle in management.

CONCLUSION

Therefore, pastoral leadership is seen both from the Scripture and the business community. Its effectiveness is evident by the number of growing churches led by aggressive pastors. My exhortation to bashful pastors is that they become more determined. To the dictators, I suggest they grow in Christian maturity, working with their deacons and people to the glory of God. "Feed the flock of God which is among you, taking the oversight thereof, not by constraint, but willingly; not for filthy lucre, but of a ready mind; Neither as being lord over God's heritage, but being ensamples to the flock" (I Pet. 5:2,3).